Hard Decisions: Forgoing and Withdrawing Artificial Nutrition and Hydration

Eileen P. Flynn

Sheed & Ward

Sheed & Ward™ is a service of National Catholic Reporter Publishing
Company, Inc.

Library of Congress Catalog Card Number: 89-63120

ISBN: 1-55612-304-3

Published by: Sheed & Ward
115 E. Armour Blvd. P.O. Box 419492
Kansas City, MO 64141-6492

To order, call: (800) 333-7373

Contents

With love and gratitude
to
Elizabeth and Luke Flynn

Introduction

As a result of modern medical technology people today are facing new and difficult ethical dilemmas. Among the most agonizing of human decisions is one which people are confronting with increasing frequency: What kinds of interventions are appropriate/inappropriate when an individual is irreversibly comatose, very ill and demented, or terminally ill, near death, and desirous for death to come soon? Patients and members of their families, ethicists, health care professionals, and hospital and nursing home administrators, as well as concerned citizens, politicians and judges, have found themselves called upon to evaluate the benefits and burdens of sustaining life via artificial feeding. The question they face is never an easy one to answer because of the complexity evident in each particular situation and the heart-rending emotional aspects of dealing with a technology which impacts directly on life and death.

This book will approach the issue of artificial nutrition and hydration from four perspectives. The first entails reviewing the medical state of the art with the intention of becoming conversant with the technology and its usage. The second involves a consideration of legal cases in order to determine the reasoning behind court decisions and the precedents which have been set by these decisions. The third area to be addressed is that of morality: What ethical principles are relevant for people who have to make decisions about initiating or discontinuing artificial nutrition and hydration? The final chapter will deal with the actual dynamics of the real life situations in which people seek to maintain their integrity while grappling with one of the most difficult decisions they will ever have to make.

This book is for the patients, surrogate decision makers, physicians, nurses, chaplains, hospital administrators and others who seek to evaluate the use, nonuse or withdrawal of artificial feeding in many different kinds of circumstances. It is also for people who want to become informed about this technology so that, should the occasion ever arise, they will be able to make knowledgeable decisions concerning it.

1

Artificial Nutrition and Hydration: An Achievement of Modern Medical Technology

Introduction

Artificial nutrition and hydration are an achievement of modern medical technology. Medical science is now able to provide sustenance to persons who are unable or unwilling to eat or drink. The feeding tubes through which the liquid components of balanced diets flow are a common feature of today's hospitals and nursing homes. Widespread availability of the technology of artificial feeding has happened only recently; as a result, people have many questions about it. In what does this technology consist? When is it used? Does it have any drawbacks? This chapter will examine the technological aspects of artificial nutrition and hydration and will consider pertinent data concerning their use. It is necessary to engage in such a review before addressing legal or moral issues attendant to artificial nutrition and hydration.

The Methods for Artificial Nutrition and Hydration

Medical techniques for artificial feeding are of two kinds, enteral and parenteral. Enteral formulas bring nutrition to a patient's gastrointestinal

1

tract. Depending on the type of tube, they enter the body at the nose, the throat, the esophagus, the stomach or the small intestine. Parenteral tube feeding, on the other hand, usually enters the body through a strong vein in the chest. Peripheral parenteral feeding is administered via smaller veins in a patient's limbs. Many of the ways modern medicine has at its disposal for providing artificial nutrition and hydration are named for the anatomical sites at which the solutions enter the human body.

Intravenous feeding and hydration. A common hospital procedure is the administration of sustenance by means of an IV line (intravenous, i.e., within a vein). Peripheral parenteral nourishment is provided on a temporary basis. Fluids are delivered directly to the bloodstream through veins in the limbs. However, it is not possible to provide a balanced diet over an extended period of time through IV tubes.

Nasogastric tubes (NG tubes). These tubes are inserted nonsurgically. A common enteral method of artificial nutrition and hydration, they are placed through the nose, down the esophagus and into the stomach.

Nasoenteral tubes (also known as Dobhoff tubes). Like NG tubes, these tubes do not require a surgical incision and they provide an adequate vehicle for enteral nutrition. Nasoenteral tubes are placed through the nose, down the esophagus, through the stomach and into either the first or second portion of the small intestine.

Pharyngostomy and Esophagostomy tubes. These tubes provide enteral nutrition and are placed through the neck, into either the throat or upper esophagus, and into the stomach. Their insertion requires surgery. (Esophagostomy tubes are rarely used.)

Gastrostomy tubes (G tubes). Enteral nutrition is brought directly to the stomach when gastrostomy tubes are employed. Gastrostomy tubes are inserted through the abdomen into the stomach by means of a surgical incision.

Jejunostomy tubes (J tubes). Jejunostomy tubes bring enteral nutrition into the jejunum (the second loop of the small intestine). Their surgical insertion is through the abdomen and directly into the small intestine.

Total Parenteral Nutrition (TPN; total parenteral nutrition is also known as hyperalimentation or central hyperalimentation). Total parenteral nutrition is infused into a large vein located beneath the clavicle (collarbone). The process of TPN requires the surgical insertion of a catheter through a subclavian vein and into the superior vena cava. The superior vena cava is a one-inch vein that returns blood to the heart from the upper part of the body. Outside the body, in the chest region, the catheter is connected to a filter and then to the tubing which transmits the intravenous solution. TPN is used for patients who do not have a functioning gastrointestinal tract, or have an increased demand for nutrition because of a debilitating illness. TPN enables very weakened patients to be fed the high caloric diets which they require.

In pediatric patients TPN is accomplished by making an incision in the infant's or child's neck or chest region and threading a catheter in two directions, first, through the jugular vein into the superior vena cava, and, second, through a tunnel under the skin of the head so that the catheter exits in back of the scalp. The catheter is connected to a filter at the point of its exit and thence to the tubing which carries a TPN formula.

Solutions Used for Artificial Sustenance

When patients are tube fed their nourishment is in liquid form. Table foods can be blenderized and fed to a person through tubes; however, blenderized feedings are not used in total parenteral nutrition. A variety of commercially prepared formulas also provide nourishment for people who are tube fed, and these are used more frequently than blenderized formulas. Sometimes, in response to the needs of individual patients, these formulas are supplemented by additional nutrients and/or vitamins. The appearance of powdered nutrition dates from the beginning of the U.S. space program; as a result of this technological development the pharmaceutical industry acquired knowledge of how to make powdered formulas for patients who are incapable of eating and drinking. Premixed formulas are reconstituted by adding water. In addition to standard formulas, there are special preparations for patients with particular needs such as kidney, liver and respiratory diseases, burn victims and pediatric patients. An Office of Technology Assessment report refers to a new development in powdered feeding formulas: Recently developed modular formulas allow the combination of individual nutrients to meet the specific needs of each patient and offer an alternative to premixed formulas.[1] Nevertheless, it is premixed formulas—without additions—which are used in the vast majority of cases.

The elemental diets which are fed to patients through feeding tubes contain sources of nitrogen which provide protein, carbohydrates for calories, a minimum amount of fatty acids, and sufficient electrolytes, trace elements and vitamins to meet human nutritional needs. These liquid diets do not require work on the part of the digestive system in order to be digested. Because they are in liquid form elemental diets are equivalent to predigested nourishment.

Several factors have to be taken into account in order to determine the specific nutritional requirements of individual patients. It is important to learn the kinds and amounts of nutrients consumed by patients when they fed themselves or were fed by mouth. Measurements of weight, lean body mass and fat stores need to be taken. If a patient is suffering from anemia, the specific nutrients which are lacking need to be determined. It is also necessary to find out the patient's white blood count so as to estimate disease-fighting potential, and to know the levels of stored vitamins and minerals. This information should be obtained before the primary physician and dietician collaborate to prescribe or design a feeding solution. While physicians and dieticians are primarily responsible for nutritional assessment and design of treatment, family members or nurses are usually the first persons to notice symptoms of malnutrition and to set in motion the series of steps which lead to artificial feeding. As we have seen, the state of the art of artificial nutrition and hydration allows for the tailoring of solutions to meet the vast range of individual requirements. However, significant numbers of people in nursing homes who are on artificial feeding and who are served by a relatively small number of dieticians are usually fed standard formulas without much attention being given to individual needs.[2]

Inserting Artificial Feeding Tubes and Difficulties Associated with Tube Feeding

Nasogastric feeding tubes are used more frequently than any other kind of tube. Their insertion does not require surgery and they can be put in place by anyone trained in the proper technique for insertion, including the patient. Ordinarily, NG tubes are left in place all the time; it is possible, however, to remove them when feeding is terminated and to reinsert them when feeding is once again initiated. The process of insertion is usually accomplished as follows: If awake and able to cooperate, the patient, in a prone or semi-prone position, is asked to swallow water repetitively as the tube, which is lubricated with a tasteless water-based jelly, is passed through the posterior pharynx and esophagus into the stomach. Because the swallowing action is often difficult to achieve, the person inserting the tube may stroke the patient's throat to help the patient to swallow. Many patients find insertion of NG tubes uncomfortable and gag while the tube is being put in place. Competent patients are less fearful and more relaxed and cooperative if they receive a thorough explanation about the procedure before it is carried out.

Sometimes confused patients are frightened at the prospect of the insertion of feeding tubes and they need to be restrained while the procedure is being carried out. In the case of an unconscious patient or an incompetent patient who is incapable of cooperation because of a condition such as dementia, the insertion of NG tubes requires considerable skill and strength on the part of the person inserting them. This person has to be experienced in judging the path the tube is taking within the patient's body so that the tube terminates in the stomach and not in a lung. In addition, the person inserting the NG tube needs to take care not to scratch or puncture any of the organs through which the tube passes and has to be prepared to respond appropriately should the patient gag or vomit. The practice of withdrawing gastric contents with a syringe immediately after the insertion of an NG tube is a test performed to make certain that the tube has been properly placed in the stomach. By expelling the contents of the syringe in water, one can ascertain whether or not this is the case. If bubbles form in the water, the syringe contains air from the patient's lung and the tube needs to be repositioned so that the patient's breathing is not impaired. A second method of checking on tube placement is by x-ray.

Patients may experience several different kinds of problems in connection with NG tubes. Conscious patients, both those who exhibit evidence of being confused and those who do not, frequently seem bothered by the nasogastric tube and try to pull it out. If these patients cannot be convinced to stop trying to remove the tube, and if NG feeding is to continue, it is necessary that they be physically restrained and their hands bound in mittens. Restrained patients are at risk of developing bedsores and pneumonia, two consequences of a dislike of nasogastric feeding; the risk of bedsores and pneumonia is lessened, however, if proper nursing procedures are followed.

Long-term placement of NG tubes may cause irritation to the nose; in its most severe form this irritation results in bleeding, or injury to nasal tissue and the nasal passage. Irritation of the throat, sometimes accompanied by vomiting, can also occur as can sinus irritation, congestion and infection. A serious complication which sometimes accompanies the use of nasogastric tubes is aspiration pneumonia caused by the accidental regurgitation of liquid nourishment destined for the gastrointestinal tract into the patient's lungs.

Nasoenteral tubes differ from nasogastric tubes in that they deliver liquid nutrition to the small intestine. The same possible complications accompany the use of nasoenteral tubes as NG tubes except that the likelihood of aspirating a feeding is very minimal. It is apparent that both restrained and nonrestrained patients who receive nutrition and hydration from nasogastric and nasoenteral tubes require extensive nursing care and diligent monitoring in order to avoid or deal with complications.

If enteral nutrition is not administered through nasogastric or nasoenteral tubes, minor surgery must be performed for the insertion of any other kind of tubing. Because surgery is required, informed voluntary consent must be procured before the procedure is carried out. Regardless of the type of feeding tube used, the insertions have many features in common. A local anesthetic is administered to the patient and an incision is made by a surgeon who guides the tip of the tube to the desired location within the patient's gastrointestinal system. The surgeon then secures the tubing with adhesive or sutures at its point of entry into the body. Gastrostomy and jejunostomy tubes tend to be more comfortable for the patient than NG tubes.

The complications which can result from surgical placement of feeding tubes include bleeding from the incision and infections of the incision and internal organs. Proper nursing care which pays particular attention to skin care at the site of the incision and frequent changes of bandages are imperative.

All the various types of tubes which are used for enteral nutrition can be misplaced within a patient's body. As we have seen, a nasogastric tube could be mistakenly inserted into a patient's lung instead of the stomach. In addition, enteral feeding tubes can become displaced after they have been in use. For example, a gastrostomy tube can become displaced and discharge its contents into the abdominal cavity instead of into the stomach.[3] Accordingly, it is necessary for those who monitor patients to check and recheck tube placement when the tube is first inserted and subsequently, and to be alert for any signs that a feeding tube may have become displaced.

Total parenteral nutrition requires a surgical procedure which is carried out under sterile conditions by a skilled physician assisted by appropriately trained personnel. The area on the patient's body where the incision is to be made needs to be prepared in advance of the procedure so that the antiseptic solutions used in conjunction with catheter insertion do not burn the patient's skin. The patient needs to be sedated but it is desirable that the patient be sufficiently alert to cooperate during the insertion by performing a breathing exercise known as the Valsalva maneuver. The physician's task is to thread a catheter through a subclavian vein and to place the tip of the catheter into the superior vena cava. The needle used for this threading is then removed and the tube-like catheter attached by adhesive or sutures at the place where it exits the body. Following the positioning of the catheter, the catheter is connected to a filter and the filter is attached to tubing.

Skill is required for the insertion of the catheter used for TPN. If the procedure is not carried out properly, it is possible to puncture a vein or a lung. A malpositioned catheter can cause phlebitis. And, as with other surgically inserted tubes, there is the possibility of an abscess developing at the catheter entry site. It is imperative that the placement of the catheter be checked by x-ray, and that additional x-rays be taken from time to time to make certain that the catheter has not moved.

From the point of view of the patient, TPN can cause a significant amount of stress. A catheter in one's chest can be annoying and frightening. Being dependent for one's life on so sophisticated a treatment can cause feelings of anxiety; there can also be feelings of resentment about being in a state of dependence. Whether the patient on TPN is in a hospital, a nursing home or at home, the patient needs the assistance of specialized physicians and nurses in order to continue to be nourished.

The various types of tubes used for enteral and parenteral nutrition need to be cleaned or changed from time to time; cleaning is accomplished by removing the tube from the patient and flushing it with water or another safe cleaning solution.

In regard to instructing patients who are going to be on tube feeding at home, the Office of Technology Assessment states:

> Nutritional support specialists agree that it usually takes about two weeks in the hospital to train patients who are going home on TPN. Training for patients going home on tube feeding usually takes 3 to 6 hours over the course of several days in the hospital. Obviously, the patient's physical, emotional and mental status affect training time.[4]

Some physicians, dieticians, pharmacists and nurses are well versed in all aspects of enteral and parenteral nutrition. Because the possibility of providing artificial sustenance to patients is a fairly recent phenomenon, many health care professionals are still unfamiliar with all the options and techniques. Programs to educate, train and assess the competence of health care practitioners are needed in order to ensure the proper usage of artificial feeding.

Frequency of Use of Artificial Sustenance and Treatment Cost

Statistics present reliable estimates of the number of people who are being artificially fed; they should not, however, be considered to be precise tabulations. These estimates, moreover, are a few years old; it is safe to assume that today more patients are being artificially fed than were in the past. According to the most recent available data, the Office of TechnologyAssessment reported that in 1984 approximately 1.4 million people received nutritional support from feeding tubes, 500,000 patients receiving TPN and 780,000 receiving enteral nutrition.[5] More than 96 percent of these patients were in hospitals. Approximately 3 percent were residents of nursing homes. According to the OTA, "Charles H. Kline Co. estimated that 53,400 nursing home residents (about 4 percent of all residents) received tube feeding and 15,600 residents (about 1 percent of all residents) received TPN in 1985."[6] Data available in 1984 and 1985 put the number of people on TPN at home at between 2,000 and 5,000; it is estimated that between 15,000 and 20,000 people received enteral nutrition at home.[7] The number of tube fed patients who are unconscious and not expected to regain consciousness ever, that is, who are in a so-called persistent vegetative state, is estimated to be between 5,000 and 10,000. While the OTA cites these figures about patients in a persistent vegetative state, it cautions that they have not been confirmed by scientific data-gathering means.[8] In the absence of scientifically gathered data, however, these figures are the only ones available and are helpful in suggesting how frequently tube feeding is used for permanently and irreversibly comatose patients.

There is considerable variation in the cost of both TPN and enteral nutrition and hydration. In regard to TPN the OTA reports:

> According to one survey, the average cost of formulas, equipment, and associated staff time for TPN for hospitalized patients in 1985 was $196 per day (range: $25 to $500) . . . . Other studies report average costs ranging from $75 to $400 a day for TPN formulas and associated staff time for hospitalized patients.[9]

The Office of Technology Assessment was unable to determine the cost of providing TPN or enteral nutrition for patients in nursing homes. In regard to how much it costs to be on TPN at home, the OTA quoted the estimate of one contractor who put the charges in the range of $50,000 to $100,000 per year.[10]

Enteral nutrition which is provided by the several different methods described above is significantly less expensive than TPN. In 1985 in the hospital setting it averaged $43 a day with a range of $4 to $132.[11] The cost of enteral nutrition at home ranges from $3,000 to $12,000 per year.[12] Blenderized feedings cost considerably less than premade formulas, but dollar estimates for blenderized feedings are unavailable.

The following chart reveals the manner in which payment for artificial sustenance is made.

Source of Payment for Parenteral and Enteral Nutrition, All Ages, All Settings, U. S., 1984.

Source of Payment	Parenteral Nutrition	Enteral Nutrition
Medicare	33%	30%
Medicaid	8%	5%
Private insurance	58%	55%
Self pay	1%	10%[13]

Indications for Artificial Feeding

Certain occurrences or disabilities indicate the need for nutrition and hydration to be administered artificially. People who are physically unable to masticate and/or swallow can benefit from enteral nutrition. Patients who have obstructions in the gastrointestinal tract, postoperative patients who cannot eat for a time following gastrointestinal surgery, and people with acute or chronic diseases who are unable to digest or absorb nutrients (this category includes some persons with AIDS) present indications for TPN. Some critically ill patients and some postoperative patients need supplemental tube feeding in order to avoid becoming malnourished and dehydrated. Patients who are comatose as well as some other classes of patients, e.g., severely demented persons, present indications for enteral feeding because, in the absence of administration of such sustenance, patients in these categories would certainly die.

Contraindications for Artificial Feeding/Hydration

In medicine, a contraindication refers to any condition of disease which makes a treatment inadvisable on medical grounds, that is, apart from moral, emotional or aesthetic considerations. The judgment that a specific procedure or medication is contraindicated is made by considering potential risks and benefits to an individual patient, taking into account that patient's unique circumstances, and reaching a decision based on the facts of a particular case. Artificially supplied nutrition and hydration are generally not considered to be medically indicated for dying patients when death is imminent. (By "imminent" is meant within a matter of hours or, at most, a day or two. This conclusion is self-evident in cases involving dying patients who are unable to absorb nutrients which could be artificially administered.) In the cases of infants who are born with unquestionably terminal diagnoses, such as anencephaly (absence of all but the brain stem) and for whom there are no possible therapeutic interventions, a futile treatment such as tube feeding is frequently assessed as medically contraindicated.

It is possible that patients may experience fever and distress as a result of abscesses which develop at the sites of surgical insertion; in such cases, reinsertion of tubes may be contraindicated. In addition, the irritation caused by nasogastric tubes and the restraints under which patients may have to be kept so that they do not pull the tubes out may prove so vexing to some patients that this manner of providing nutrition and hydration may come to be regarded as contraindicated.

Medical Advances, Especially Those in Artificial Feeding, Lead to New Ethical Questions

Approximately two million people die each year in the United States. The illnesses causing mortality most often are heart disease (34%), malignancies (22%), and cerebrovascular disease

(7%). Traumatic death—including accidents, homicide and suicide—account for 13% of all deaths. Only the relatively few who die very suddenly from accident, heart attack, or stroke are likely to have been without medical attention.[14]

In the United States the way people die has changed. At the turn of this century the majority of people died of incurable communicable diseases, accidents and injuries. In spite of the increasing incidence of AIDS, most people today do not die of communicable diseases; neither do they die quickly. Diagnoses of such ailments as cancer, heart disease, kidney disease and a variety of other degenerative afflictions are usually paired with one or more treatment options. As a result of the technology which has given us sophisticated diagnostic tools, antibiotics, radiation therapy, chemotherapy, pacemakers, open heart surgery, dialysis, and many other procedures, both experimental and nonexperimental, most people now take an active part in determining how the final phase of their lives will be managed.

A second difference in the way people die today concerns the status of the dying person in regard to nutrition and hydration. Up until very recently malnutrition and dehydration accompanied every death that followed an illness of more than a few days duration. Caretakers did what they could to keep dying persons comfortable. Ice chips and sips of water were offered, and petroleum jelly or lemon glycerine were used to moisten lips. But there was no way to nourish dying patients with sufficient calories and to hydrate them with enough fluids to prevent malnutrition and dehydration. Given the scope of this study, it is important to understand the nature of malnutrition and dehydration. The Office of Technology Assessment offers the following definitions:

Malnutrition is a condition caused by inadequate intake of calories, protein, carbohydrates, fat, vitamins, minerals, trace elements, or any combination thereof .... the effects include weight loss, listlessness, and depression; decreased ability to resist infection, to recover from illness and to withstand surgery or other treatments; impaired wound healing; decreased cardiac and respiratory muscle strength, confusion, coma, and eventual death.

Dehydration, the loss of body water in excess of intake, is caused by decreased fluid intake or inability to conserve fluids as a result, for example, of renal disease or severe diarrhea. Dehydration results in dry mucous membranes; decreased sweat, saliva, and tears; muscle weakness, rigidity or tremors; confusion, hallucinations, and delirium; abnormal respiration; coma; and eventual death. Reduced body water also alters the concentration of electrolytes such as sodium and potassium, with severe and sometimes life-threatening consequences.[15]

While these definitions convey a stark notion of malnutrition and dehydration as a very uncomfortable state of being, there are two instances in which this may not be the case. The first concerns patients who are in a persistent vegetative state. Excerpts from the statement of the American Academy of Neurology in regard to what a persistent vegetative state is and what patients in this condition are capable of experiencing are informative in this regard:

> The persistent vegetative state is a form of eyes-open permanent unconsciousness in which the patient has periods of wakefulness and physiologic sleep/wake cycles, but at no time is the patient aware of himself or his environment. Neurologically, being awake, but unaware is the result of a functioning brainstem, and the total loss of cerebral cortical functioning. . . .

> Persistent vegetative state patients do not have the capacity to experience pain or suffering. Pain and suffering are attributes of consciousness requiring cerebral cortical functioning, and patients who are permanently and completely unconscious cannot experience these symptoms.[16]

In regard to another class of patients for whom malnutrition and dehydration might actually be beneficial, Rebecca S. Dresser, J.D., and Eugene Boisaubin, Jr., M.D., relate their clinical observation:

> . . . dehydration can reduce the patient's secretions and excretions, thus decreasing breathing problems, vomiting, and incontinence. Dehydration usually leads to death through hemoconcentration and hyperosmolality with subsequent azotemia, hypernatremia,

and hypercalcemia. All of these produce sedative effects on the brain just before death. If quality of dying is analyzed in a manner similar to quality of life, then many terminally ill patients might prefer dehydration over other ways to die.[17]

If Dresser and Boisaubin are correct about the sedative effects of dehydration on the brain, there is reason to reexamine the assumption that dehydration is generally undesirable. The experience of Phyllis Schmitz, R.N., and Merry O'Brien, R.N., of the Washington Home Hospice in Washington, D.C., provides further reason not to think of dehydration in exclusively negative terms:

> We have not seen evidence that dehydration occurring at the termination of life results in any pain or distressing experience for the patient. To the contrary, even patients who remain quite alert and communicative become objectively dehydrated without substantial symptoms when treated for dry mouth.[18]

Just as, in general, the cause of death is different today from what it was a few generations ago, so, too, the place where people die has changed. The deathbed used to be a place around which generations of family members gathered to pass the final hours with a dying relative. Neighbors, friends and associates were accustomed to stop by and bid farewell to the dying person. There is speculation that death was less fearsome for our forebears because it was closer to them. Whether or not this speculation is accurate, there is no question that since the end of World War II dying has become more and more institutionalized. In 1949, 58 percent of deaths occurred in hospitals and nursing homes; in 1958 the figure was 61 percent; in 1977, 70 percent; and, today, approximately 80 percent of people face a prolonged institutionalized dying.[19]

In the 1980s artificial nutrition and hydration are a standard feature of the medical care found in hospitals and nursing homes. Various kinds of tube feeding are becoming more and more available to the increasing numbers of patients who are at risk of malnutrition and dehydration. How is it that technology has brought us so far so fast?

Total parenteral nutrition dates from 1968. An American physician, Dr. Stanley Dudrick, adapted a technique developed by the French surgeon

Aubaniac and accomplished the feat of providing nourishment to patients who had nonfunctioning gastrointestinal tracts. In the early 1950's Aubaniac introduced subclavian venipuncture (a surgical incision into a large vein located under the collarbone) as a means of rapidly administering blood to soldiers wounded on the field of battle. Dr. Dudrick benefitted from the engineering model implemented by Aubaniac. At first he worked in a laboratory to design and synchronize the components for TPN; then he tested total parenteral nutrition on animals. By 1968 Dudrick's system was ready for human use. Its parts—a needle for inserting a catheter, the catheter, a filter, IV tubing, a plastic sac-like bag containing liquid nourishment, a pump to regulate the rate of infusion, powdered formulas and a method for their sterile preparation—had been designed and coordinated, and could be offered to human patients. The individual components have undergone changes and development through the years but the basic system designed by Dudrick remains unaltered.

At the outset TPN was practiced in only a few large hospitals. At the present time it is widely available and, as we have seen, is even used at home by a growing number of patients. A comment by Dr. David Major reveals why TPN came into widespread usage:

> In the 1970s it became clear that the process of total parenteral nutrition had become a mainstay for helping critically ill patients survive acute illnesses where the prognosis had previously been near hopeless.[20]

Providing patients with enteral nutrition was possible centuries before the birth of Christ. Egyptian and Greek physicians used syringes to deliver liquid nutrition to the rectum. Only about 400 calories per day could be absorbed in this way and, because of predictable irritation to the rectum, this method could be used for just a brief time. Attempts at enteral nutrition using surgical access through the stomach, duodenum and intestine date from the late sixteenth century with a variety of catheters, syringes and tubes (made of rubber or leather) used to carry out the procedure. Beginning in the second half of the nineteenth century, some patients received feeding through the nose. In 1910 M. Einhorn published a report of a major improvement in gastrostomy feeding; Einhorn's rubber tube could deliver nutrients for as long as 8-12 days. Accounts of various forms of enteral nutrition through the mid 1940s relate that this form of feeding was administered mainly to postoperative patients and was generally of short-term duration. In the 1950s patients with anorexia, terminal cancer and duodenal fistula began to be treated with enteral feeding. It was not until the 1970s that tube feeding became generally available in major medical centers throughout the United States. Although some coma patients were tube fed in the 1950s, this was not a routine practice until the mid to late 1970s.[21]

The most significant clinical breakthrough with regard to enteral nutrition as we know it today is attributed to direction given by M.D. Pareira in his monograph, *Therapeutic Nutrition with Tube Feeding*, published in 1959. In this connection Henry T. Randall writes:

> [Pareira] emphasized the relationship that exists between starvation and anorexia, and the importance of breaking the cycle that leads to malnutrition by therapeutic intervention by tube feeding. He stated that tube feeding guarantees certainty of intake, with respect to both calories and balance of nutrients.

Pareira's recommendations—use of a small caliber (2.5 mm or less) soft tube, initial feeding by continuous drip or pump, the use of dilute feeding formula for several days to permit adaptation, and emphasis on the importance of access to free water for drinking or provision of extra water by tube—are all principles that are completely applicable to modern enteral nutrition.[22]

During the past few decades, the development of powdered formulas which are reconstituted by the addition of water as well as the availability of ready to use liquid diets have made enteral nutrition simpler and more convenient. Improvements in the manufacture of plastics so that lightweight, soft and very flexible materials are now available for nasogastric and nasoenteral tubes are also significant. So, too, is the fact that pumps have been perfected which can control the rate of infusion and which avoid the dual problems of infusion which is too fast or too slow.

There is no question that artificial nutrition is a familiar therapy in the modern hospital or nursing home. The pharmaceutical industry has expanded to provide the materials used in enteral and parenteral nutrition.

Dieticians have developed the expertise to recommend appropriate liquid diets for patients who are unable or unwilling to take food by mouth. As a result of medical advances, there are large numbers of such patients. Instruction and training about artificial sustenance are now included in the curricula of many medical schools and are also available "on the job." As a result, in a relatively short period of time medical technology has developed several remarkable processes for artificial nutrition and hydration.

In view of the fact that it is possible to nourish people who cannot eat or drink, members of the medical and legal professions, ethicists, religious leaders, lawmakers, and a growing number of interested lay people are beginning to discuss some questions which have arisen as a result of the new technology. The most basic issue is in regard to the nature of parenteral and enteral nutrition: Are these procedures equivalent to providing food and drink, or should they be evaluated as medical treatments? And, does their provision constitute basic, nondispensable supportive or nursing care? The other major issue concerns incompetent patients, both those who are diagnosed as terminally ill and close to death and those who are in a so-called persistent vegetative state. Should the last days or months of life be extended by the artificial provision of nutrition and hydration? Does artificial sustenance provide comfort to the patient? What should be done on behalf of a patient who has suffered extensive brain damage and for whom medical science holds out no hope of recovery from coma? These are today's questions; with the growing availability of artificial nutrition and hydration, more questions will likely be added in the years ahead.

Conclusion

Artificial nutrition and hydration can be delivered to the gastrointestinal system (enteral nutrition) or can be infused directly into the bloodstream (total parenteral nutrition). Skill is required for the insertion of feeding tubes; nasogastric or nasoenteral tubes are put in place by a properly trained physician, nurse or lay person. A physician is needed to make the incision for any other type of tube. Both parenteral and enteral nutrition are expensive, with the former being far more so than the latter. Artificial nutrition and hydration are indicated when a patient is unable or unwilling to eat or drink. Nutritional support through artificial feeding represents a significant benefit for the vast majority of patients who lack the ability to take food and drink orally. However, nearness to death, hopelessness of prognosis or difficulties experienced in conjunction with the use of feeding tubes may constitute contraindications to their use. Today's ethical issues attendant to feeding tubes tend to focus on the appropriateness of their use for persons who are diagnosed as irreversibly comatose or who have suffered other forms of permanent brain impairment.

Endnotes

1. Congress of the United States, Office of Technology Assessment, "Life-Sustaining Technologies and the Elderly," July 31, 1987, p. 280.

2. Ibid., pp. 298, 299.

3. Ibid., p. 282.

4. Ibid., p. 302.

5. Ibid., p. 293.

6. Ibid., p. 297. (Charles H. Kline Co. is a pharmaceutical firm which is involved in the manufacture of materials used for artificial feeding.)

7. Ibid., p. 300.

8. Ibid., p. 298.

9. Ibid., p. 295.

10. Ibid., p. 303.

11. Ibid., p. 295.

12. Ibid., p. 303.

13. Ibid., p. 296.

14. President's Commission for the Study of Ethical Problems in Medicine and Biomedical and Behavioral Research, *Deciding to Forgo Life-Sustaining Treatment* (Washington, DC: U.S. Government Printing Office, 1983), p. 15.

15. OTA, p. 278.

16. American Academy of Neurology, Position Statement, Minneapolis, MN, 1989.

17. Rebecca S. Dresser, J.D., and Eugene V. Boisaubin, Jr., M.D., "Ethics, Law, and Nutritional Support," *Archives of Internal Medicine*, 145, January, 1985, p. 124.

18. Phyllis Schmitz and Merry O'Brien, "Observations on Nutrition and Hydration in Dying Cancer Patients," in Joanne Lynn, M.D., *By No Extraordinary Means* (Bloomington, IN: Indiana University Press, 1986), p. 36.

19. President's Commission, pp. 17-18.

20. David Major, M.D., "The Medical Procedures for Providing Food and Water: Indications and Effects," in Lynn, p. 24.

21. Henry T. Randall, "The History of Enteral Nutrition," in John L. Rombeau, M.D., and Michael D. Caldwell, M.D., Ph.D., *Enteral and Tube Feeding* (Philadelphia, PA: W.B. Saunders Co., 1984), p. 8. My survey sketch of the development of enteral nutrition follows Randall's development, pp. 1-9.

22. Ibid., p. 7.

2
Legal Aspects of the Question

Introduction

Modern medical technology has made it possible to provide nutrition and hydration to patients who cannot or will not eat and drink. Artificial sustenance is beneficial for the majority of patients who receive it. The liquid nourishment which is pumped through plastic tubes, as well as the means of providing the nourishment, i.e. the tubes themselves, are beneficial because they keep patients alive and frequently make possible the return to a normal life. That is, most patients on tube feeding can look forward to the resumption of eating and drinking as well as the restoration of their health.

It is apparent that technology is used well when it is used to serve human needs. Questions about the appropriateness of the use of artificial nutrition and hydration arise when it is unclear whether or not the best interests of a particular patient are being served or when there is uncertainty concerning what course of action (nonaction) constitutes a proper exercise of professional responsibility by physicians, nurses or health care administrators. Several recent cases provide examples of confusion and tension surrounding the use of artificial nutrition and hydration. These cases, and the legal analyses which accompanied them, attracted attention from the public-at-large and, especially, from the media. As a result of this interest, consciousness has been raised concerning the existence and possible uses of artificial feeding and popular and scholarly discussion of the technology and its desirable usage have increased.

• Did it serve the interests of Paul E. Brophy, a patient in a persistent vegetative state, to prevent his death by providing him with artificial nutrition and hydration in contradiction to the wishes he expressed when competent? His physicians thought it did, but his wife was convinced that it did not. Court intervention was necessary to resolve the dispute.

• Claire C. Conroy, an elderly and senile nursing home patient whose aversion for medical procedures was established, was fed by nasogastric tubes. Did her feeding tube benefit Ms. Conroy or did the fact that the NG tube was probably experienced as disagreeable and uncomfortable signify that the tube was not a benefit and should not be used? Physicians and nursing home administrators considered NG tube feeding a reasonable therapy for Ms. Conroy; her nephew disagreed. Recourse to the courts was necessary to settle the matter.

• Mary O'Connor, an elderly nursing home patient, was disabled as a result of suffering several strokes. Mrs. O'Connor was conscious, could feel pain, respond to simple commands and carry on very limited conversations. She could not, however, articulate her feelings about being fed by an NG tube. Her daughters, both nurses, sought to honor their mother's previously expressed wishes by having her nasogastric feeding terminated. Physicians were reluctant to grant their request. The New York Court of Appeals ultimately resolved the deadlock.

• At the request of the patient's wife, Neil Barber, M.D., and Robert Nejdl, M.D., removed a feeding tube from Clarence Herbert, a patient who had suffered irreversible brain damage, and Mr. Herbert died. One of the nurses who cared for Mr. Herbert alerted the district attorney's office regarding what she considered an act of malpractice on the part of the physicians. The district attorney brought charges of homicide against them. Intervention by the Court of Appeals of the State of California was necessary to evaluate the action of the physicians in ordering removal of the feeding tube.

• Would a health care facility be acting in an upright manner or assisting in a suicide by providing pain medication to a competent, conscious adult patient who tired of living as a paraplegic and desired to starve herself to death under medical supervision? Such was the dilemma raised by Elizabeth Bouvia in 1983. The Superior Court of the State of California for the County of Riverside deliberated on this case in order to reach a response. Subsequently, in 1986, while in the High Desert Hospital, a healthcare facility in the County of Los Angeles, California, Elizabeth Bouvia willingly ingested a limited soft diet by mouth but refused to grant authorization for a nasogastric tube. In spite of her express instructions the medical staff at the hospital inserted a nasogastric tube against her will. Ms. Bouvia turned to the courts for support of her right to refuse unwanted medical treatment.

• The November, 1988 decision of the Supreme Court of Missouri in the case of Nancy Cruzan was appealed to the United States Supreme Court and the Supreme Court agreed to hear the case. A decision is likely in 1990. Will the U.S. Supreme Court uphold the reasoning of the highest Missouri court that Ms. Cruzan, who has been in a persistent vegetative state since surviving a 1983 automobile accident, should be fed by gastrostomy tube, or will it agree with Ms. Cruzan's parents who request discontinuance of artificial feeding, a medical treatment which they contend brings no benefit to their daughter?

What can be learned from the difficult cases which have been heard during the 1980s? The reasoning set forth by the justices who deliberated on each case, as well as the precedents which have been set as a result of their decisions, serve both to inform and instruct American society on many ethical aspects of the use and withdrawal of artificial sustenance. While there is a strong connection between law and ethics, courts do not *decide* what is right and what is wrong. They attempt *to understand* in what right and wrong conduct consist so as to base their decisions on sound moral principles and to prescribe ethically defensible courses of conduct. Courts in the United States are especially sensitive to medical ethics because they consider themselves required to safeguard the ethical standards of the medical profession. In the context of the interface between law and ethics it is interesting to note that the role of the courts in decisions which relate to the exercise of self-determination is to ensure the right of an individual to elect or reject any medical treatment and not to dictate that a person be guided by any particular moral standard in reaching the decision.

The Context in which Legal Cases Are Decided

When a case concerning the forgoing or withdrawing of artificial feeding goes before a court, the task of the justices is to weigh arguments, principles and options in order to decide upon the right course of action. Past cases have dealt with patients' rights to refuse treatment, circumstances under which it is appropriate for a surrogate to speak on behalf of an incompetent, the obligations of medical professionals and interests the state is required to protect. In cases regarding the provision of artificial sustenance, substantial arguments are usually presented by the conflicting parties. In addition, one option is usually certain to result in death, i.e. in cases involving patients who have suffered a permanent loss of ability to swallow. Accordingly, cases about artificial feeding are very difficult and controversial.

Justices do not possess formulas, insights or norms which are unavailable to lay people. Selected to serve society, ideally they should be members of society who are clear thinkers and who have significant competence in interpreting the law. They need to be balanced and impartial. Justices learn their values and ethics in the communities from which they come. If moral consensus regarding particular practices has not yet been reached by society, it often falls to the judiciary to play a key role in articulating what might best represent such a consensus. In regard to use and non-use of artificial feeding, U. S. courts have been playing just such a role.

When the United States was established, the Constitution was adopted and the Bill of Rights was soon added. In the United States the tradition of respecting and insuring individual rights has a long and honored history. Twentieth century medical technology presents justices with the challenge of determining how the explicit Constitutional right to privacy along with the common law right to self-determination impact on incompetent patients whose next of kin request discontinuance of tube feeding. Judicial decisions reached in the United States attempt to be faithful to the unique context of the tradition of individual rights established by the Constitution and our legal heritage founded on English common law.

In addition to attending to the rights of particular individuals, justices must also pay heed to a second aspect of the decisions they reach. The state has an interest in respecting the biological life of vulnerable patients, safe-guarding the integrity of the medical profession, and insuring that institutions such as hospitals and nursing homes are free to act in conformity with their moral standards. Resolving the tensions which sometimes arise as a result of conflicts between concern for individual rights and the need to preserve the common good may result in division among justices as is evidenced by the issuance of majority and minority opinions. Even when a court reaches a consensus, difficulty can be experienced in achieving a balance which respects both the interests of individual plaintiffs and those of the state.

In regard to cases which arise in conjunction with the possibilities of sophisticated biomedical technology, many professional, religious and citizen groups are eager to offer insight and analysis. They do this by submitting briefs (position papers) to the courts for their consideration. In the course of their deliberations justices review the perspectives and reasoning of these groups and try to honor the compelling principles which are presented.

Prior to the 1980s there were no court cases explicitly dealing with forgoing or withdrawing artificial feeding. As a result, justices who heard the first cases had to decide them without reference to precedents from cases characterized by similar facts. This does not mean that no guidance was available from other kinds of cases. On the contrary, precedents set in cases about the rights of persons intent on suicide, removal of respirators, and refusals of medical treatments were instructive. Even though such instruction is informative, justices still have had to plow new ground in dealing with the intricacies of cases involving feeding tubes.

Let us consider some representative cases.

The Brophy Case

Paul E. Brophy was born on April 27, 1937. He was a healthy, robust man who worked two jobs; his main employment was as a firefighter for the town of Easton, Massachusetts. In his spare time Paul Brophy enjoyed deer hunting, fishing, gardening, and performing household chores. Married to Patricia E. Brophy, he was the father of five children.

On March 22, 1983 Paul Brophy suffered a subarachnoid hemorrhage as a result of a ruptured basilar tip aneurysm. Surgery to repair the rupture was unsuccessful; Paul Brophy did not regain consciousness following the operation. All attempts at rehabilitation ended in failure. Paul Brophy was able to breathe on his own, but had to be tube fed. At first he was fed by a nasogastric tube but, after several months, surgery was performed and a gastrostomy tube was put in place.

The damage to the brain which Paul Brophy suffered was described as serious and irreversible.[1] Because of the extensive brain damage, Paul Brophy was unable to communicate in any way, demonstrated no purposeful movement, and was unable to provide for any of his basic needs; he was diagnosed as being in a persistent vegetative state.[2] In spite of this diagnosis, Brophy's general health was good and it was possible that he might live for many years.

Because there was no change in her husband's condition during 1984, and, after "long and agonizing research,"[3] Patricia Brophy decided to request that a member of the hospital staff at the New England Sinai Hospital, Inc., remove the G tube and allow her husband to die. All five Brophy children as well as Paul Brophy's 91 year old mother and his seven siblings concurred with this decision. In reaching and affirming the decision, family members felt that they were honoring Paul Brophy's well known wishes. Although he had never given explicit directions regarding giving consent for the surgical insertion of a gastrostomy tube, he had made it very clear that he wanted the plug pulled if he were ever in a coma. And, ironically, just before his surgery he told one of his children, "If I can't sit up to kiss one of my beautiful daughters, I may as well be six foot under."

Because physicians and administrators did not agree that termination of feeding was a morally appropriate choice, Patricia Brophy took her request to the Probate and Family Court Department of the Norfolk Court. This court decided in favor of the hospital and denied Mrs. Brophy's request that artificial nutrition and hydration be terminated. It reasoned that it was good to prevent Paul Brophy's death and that the G tube was noninvasive, nonintrusive and caused no pain or suffering. The court considered the quality of the treatment furnished to Brophy more pertinent than the quality of Brophy's life, and said that the absence of objective criteria for making quality of life decisions precluded the court's involvement in such discussions. In addition, the court opined that

> A society which rejects euthanasia, the selective killing of the unfit, the insane, the retarded and the comatose patient is morally obligated to sustain the life of an ill human being, even one in a persistent vegetative state, provided that in the process of sustaining his life, he is not subjected to treatment which is highly invasive and burdensome, and which causes him extreme discomfort and pain.[4]

The Norfolk Probate Court acknowledged that it reached its decision "irrespective of the substituted judgment of the patient."[5] Mrs. Brophy appealed the Probate Court decision to the Massachusetts Supreme Judicial Court which on September 1, 1986, overturned the decision of the Probate Court by a 4-3 majority and allowed for removal of the gastrostomy tube.[6] Since the United States Supreme Court declined to review the decision, it stood.

The majority decision was based on the fact that in Paul Brophy's case there was no hope for recovery; the court was also influenced by the wishes Paul Brophy expressed when competent. In differing with the lower court, it reasoned that a patient's wishes should be honored and noted the right of a patient to refuse medical treatments even when these are clearly beneficial. The court evaluated the surgically implanted G tube as intrusive and said that gastrostomy tube feeding of a patient in a persistent vegetative state constitutes extraordinary care. Refusing to take the position that tube feeding should not be withdrawn after it has been begun, the court reasoned that such a stance could lead to unfortunate premature decisions. As far as the state's interests in regard to the welfare of Paul Brophy were concerned, the court considered a patient's right to self-determination more compelling than any interest of the state. It also held that physicians and administrators of the New England Sinai Hospital should not be required to withdraw treatment since such an action was contrary to their view of their ethical duty to their patients. Therefore, Mrs. Brophy would have to arrange the transfer of her husband to a facility which would agree to the treatment plan she advocated.

The three justices who dissented from the majority decision offered strong criticism of it. Arguments were put forward that the state interest in the preservation of life had not been given proper weight, that the right to commit or assist in suicide had been sanctioned, and that a balance which favored death over life had been struck.

The different approaches of the Probate Court and the Supreme Judicial Court as well as the significant points of conflict between the majority and minority on the Supreme Judicial Court indicate what a complex task justices face when called upon to resolve cases pertaining to the withdrawal of artificial sustenance.

Paul E. Brophy died peacefully on October 23, 1986, eight days after his feeding tube was disconnected. His final treatment plan called for supportive care including anticonvulsants and antacids. Mrs Brophy, a nurse by profession, was an active participant in designing this plan for her husband's treatment. She and her children were at Paul Brophy's bedside when he died.

The Conroy Case

Claire C. Conroy, an 84 year old nursing home resident, died on February 15, 1983. Even though she was deceased, the Supreme Court of New Jersey decided to consider the substantial issue of removal of feeding tubes from patients like Ms. Conroy, that is, those "with serious and irreversible physical and mental impairments and a limited life expectancy."[7]

Claire Conroy was admitted to Parkview Nursing Home in 1979. During her life she had been close to her three sisters, all of whom had died; she never married and had few friends. While in the nursing home she became increasingly confused, disoriented and physically dependent. Because Ms. Conroy lacked the capacity to make decisions for herself, her nephew, Thomas Whittemore, served as her guardian.

Ms. Conroy was hospitalized in 1982 due to an elevated temperature and dehydration. Diagnostic evaluation showed that her left foot was gangrenous. Two orthopedic surgeons recommended that it be amputated; they said that Ms. Conroy would die without amputation. Thomas Whittemore refused to give consent for the surgery because he felt certain that his aunt would not have wanted it. Ms. Conroy did not have the surgery and, contrary to the physicians' prognosis, she did not die from the gangrene.

Because, while hospitalized, Ms. Conroy was not getting enough nourishment by mouth she was fed by a nasogastric tube. NG feeding continued when she returned to the nursing home and Thomas Whittemore requested that Dr. Ahmed Kazemi, his aunt's physician, remove the feeding tube. His reason was that his aunt, if competent, "would not have allowed [the nasogastric tube] to be inserted in the first place."[8]

Dr. Kazemi refused to consent to Mr. Whittemore's request; the administration and staff of the nursing home remained neutral. In order to resolve the stalemate Mr. Whittemore brought an action to obtain a court order allowing removal of the tube. A trial court, the Superior Court, Chancery Division of Essex County, handed down a decision in favor of Mr. Whittemore. On appeal to the Superior Court, Appellate Division, the decision was reversed. On January 17, 1985 the Supreme Court of New Jersey handed down a decision which outlined procedures according to which artificial feeding of incompetent nursing home patients could be withdrawn. Interestingly, in view of the court's standards, Claire Conroy's nasogastric feeding could not have been discontinued because "evidence in the instant case did not meet any of the three tests for termination of life sustaining treatment."[9]

Claire Conroy was different from Paul Brophy in that she was not comatose or in a persistent vegetative state. She was cared for in a nursing home, not a hospital and her attitude concerning employment of sophisticated medical technology to keep her alive could only be inferred because it had not been explicitly stated. The aversion she felt toward doctors and medical procedures when competent was easily established, but this aversion did not necessarily mean that she would choose death over tube feeding in the present circumstances. In addition, Ms. Conroy belonged to a particular class of patients—once competent, elderly, vulnerable, presently incompetent nursing home residents who would probably die within one year—whom the state had an obvious interest in protecting. In handing down the decision that a surrogate may direct forgoing or withdrawal of artificial feeding if certain criteria are met, the court's decision is instructive in two regards: first, its explanation of why a patient has the right to refuse treatment and, second, the standards it sets to insure the integrity of surrogate decision making.

The court reasoned that patients have the right to refuse treatment based on the common law principle that men and women are free to exercise control over their bodies. In support of this stance the court quoted Judge Cooley's famous dictum: "The right to one's person may be said to be a right of complete immunity: to be let alone."[10] The court noted that surgery which is performed without consent is considered an act of assault on the surgeon's part, underscoring the respect the law pays to informed voluntary consent. In addition, the court reviewed how the right to privacy which is protected by the U. S. Constitution has been interpreted to allow married couples to use contraceptives (Griswold v. Connecticut, 1965), a woman's decision to terminate a pregnancy (Roe v. Wade, 1973), and the disconnecting of a respirator from a patient in a persistent vegetative state (In re Quinlan, 1976). The court maintained that the right to privacy also encompasses the right to refuse artificial feeding. Finally, the Supreme Court of New Jersey asserted that the right of a competent person to refuse any medical treatment, including artificial feeding, does not cease if the person becomes incompetent.

A second and very significant aspect of the decision "In the Matter of Claire C. Conroy" consists in the court's delineation of the procedure to be followed in order to determine the will of incompetent nursing home patients whose circumstances are similar to Ms. Conroy's. At the outset the court requires that two physicians concur on the diagnosis of incompetence. After such concurrence, the court prescribes that one of three tests be met: A subjective test, a limited-objective test or a pure-objective test.

The "subjective test" consists in determining if "it is clear that the patient would have refused treatment under the circumstances involved."[11] How are we to arrive at such clarity? In order to meet the subjective test the court requires considerable evidence. A document such as a living will would satisfy these requirements, provided that there was no question as to its applicability in the present circumstances. The court declared that evidence put forward by a surrogate should be tested in regard to its remoteness, consistency, thoughtfulness, maturity and specificity,[12] thus placing a considerable burden of proof on persons like Thomas Whittemore who serve as guardians for incompetents. In addition, the court said that a surrogate should be able to provide complete and accurate information about a patient's physical, sensory, emotional and cognitive functioning, degree of pain with and without treatment, life expectancy and treatment options at the time of the request to withhold or withdraw artificial feeding.[13]

If a patient's wishes cannot be determined, the court recommends either the "limited-objective test" or the "pure-objective test." The limited-objective test requires some trustworthy evidence that the incompetent patient would have refused treatment along with evidence that the burdens of a prolonged life "markedly outweigh" the "physical pleasure, emotional enjoyment, or intellectual satisfaction" life might still hold.[14] (There was controversy concerning Claire Conroy's capacity for pleasure and experience of pain; therefore, it could not be established that her being kept alive by being fed artificially was more of a burden than a benefit to her.)

When there is no evidence of what an incompetent patient would want, the Supreme Court of New Jersey requires that a pure-objective test be satisfied. This test consists in demonstrating that the burdens of treatment "clearly and markedly outweigh the benefits," and "the recurring unavoidable and severe pain of the patient's life with treatment should be such that the effect of administering life-sustaining treatment would be inhumane."[15] (An example of how life sustaining treatment consisting of artificial feeding could be/become inhumane would be in the case of a patient who had to be restrained to receive nasogastric feeding, repeatedly aspirated the feeding, then was fed by a G tube, but developed recurring infections at the site of the incision and also suffered as a result of G tube displacement. In such a case, the burdens of artificial feeding, per se, might be evaluated as greater than the benefits.)

In the mid 1970s the State of New Jersey established the Office of the Ombudsman for the Institutionalized Elderly. In the Conroy decision the Supreme Court of New Jersey prescribed the oversight of an ombudsman whenever the subjective test, the limited-objective test or the pure-objective test are used so as to avoid instances of abuse. This oversight is carried out solely by the office of the ombudsman; no court involvement is needed. (Even though avoidance of abuse to nursing home patients is a laudable goal, the oversight of the ombudsman is controversial because, in practice, it is very cumbersome.)

The O'Connor Case

At this writing Mary O'Connor is an incompetent 77 year old widowed nursing home patient; her incompetence resulted from a series of strokes which began in July, 1985 and which caused irreversible brain damage. After her first major stroke, Mrs. O'Connor was cared for at home by her daughters for more than two years. When, following a second major stroke in 1987, Mrs. O'Connor became far more disabled, she was placed in a nursing home.

On June 20, 1988 Mary O'Connor was hospitalized because she was "stuperous [sic], virtually not responsive" and had developed a fever.[16] While hospitalized she was treated for dehydration and sepsis and she was diagnosed as probably having pneumonia. In addition, upon examination it was determined that she had lost her gag reflex "making it impossible for her to swallow food or liquids without medical assistance."[17] Because she could not swallow Mrs. O'Connor was provided with nutrition and hydration by means of intravenous feeding. Since peripheral parenteral nutrition is inadequate for long-term use, her physician, Dr. Sivak, requested permission from her daughters to feed Mary O'Connor with a nasogastric tube. Seeking to honor their mother's previously expressed wishes, the daughters refused permission. The case was reviewed by the hospital ethics committee which concurred with the physician that the patient should receive artificial feeding. Since Mrs. O'Connor's daughters would not change their minds, court intervention became necessary.

Before we look at the court decision and the reasoning behind it, let us consider why Helen A. Hall and Joan Fleming, Mrs. O'Connor's daughters, did not consent to emplacement of the nasogastric tube. Helen Hall and Joan Fleming refused to consent to their mother's being artificially fed because they wanted to honor the wishes which she had expressed to them over the years. On various occasions Mrs. O'Connor had said that she did not want to be a burden, that she did not want to be kept alive by machines, that nature should be allowed to take its course, that it was monstrous to keep someone alive by artificial means, and that she did not want to lose her dignity before she passed away. When she was released from the hospital following treatment for congestive heart failure in 1984, Mrs. O'Connor said that she hoped that she would never have to go back to the hospital.

(It should be noted that Mrs. O'Connor was familiar with hospital procedures, having worked at Jacobi Hospital, Bronx, New York, for several years. In addition, she knew first hand what was involved in caring for the terminally ill, having cared for her husband and other relatives when they were dying of cancer.)

The trial court to which the Westchester County Medical Center brought its request to artificially feed Mary O'Connor denied the application. The Appellate Division affirmed the decision of the trial court. On October 14, 1988, however, the State of New York Court of Appeals reversed the order of the Appellate Division and granted the hospital's petition. Five justices concurred in the decision, and two dissented.

The difficulty encountered in honoring substitute judgment is easily uncovered through analyzing the reasoning of the majority and minority opinions in the O'Connor case. So are the problems inherent in a court's making assessments of a patient's condition and taking positions in respect to an appropriate course of action.

The majority and minority differed in regard to Mrs. O'Connor's condition. The majority concluded on the basis of the testimony of two physicians (Dr. Sivak, the treating physician, and Dr. Wasserman, a neurologist and expert witness for Hall and Fleming) that the limited amount of nourishment and antibiotics which had been administered intravenously in June, 1988 were of benefit to Mrs. O'Connor. "She showed marked improvement . . . . Within a few days she became alert, able to follow simple commands and respond verbally to simple questions."[18] In regard to her overall condition, the majority concluded from the testimony of Mary O'Connor's physicians that in spite of the substantial brain damage she had suffered she was conscious, somewhat alert, and able to respond to painful stimuli. The majority also thought that it might be possible for Mrs. O'Connor to experience an overall improvement in her condition.[19]

The majority decided on the basis of the medical data presented to them that Mrs. O'Connor's loss of a gag reflex might be temporary,[20] that she did not have a terminal illness, and that she should be regarded as

... simply an elderly person who as a result of several strokes suffers certain disabilities, including an inability to feed herself or eat in a normal manner. She is in a stable condition and if properly nourished will remain in that condition unless some other medical problem arises. Because of her age and general physical condition, her life expectancy is not great.[21]

In the minority dissent a different overall assessment of Mrs. O'Connor's medical condition emerges. Drawing on the same physician testimony the dissenting justices held that Mary O'Connor was "severely demented" and "profoundly incapacitated."[22] It was noted that she responded only sporadically to simple questions or commands, and then frequently inappropriately, and that "no hope exists for improvement in her mental or physical condition."[23] The dissenting justices evaluated Mrs. O'Connor's loss of a gag reflex as "a substantial loss of a bodily function, analogous to a patient's loss of kidney function requiring dialysis to sustain life or the inability to breathe without the aid of a respirator."[24] They concluded that Mary O'Connor

... is dying because she has suffered severe injuries to her brain and body which, if nature takes its course, will result in death. Full medical intervention will not cure or improve her, it will only maintain her in a rudimentary state of existence.[25]

In regard to interpreting the requirement that an incompetent patient's wishes as expressed when competent should be honored, both the majority and minority agreed that this ought to be the case. There was substantial disagreement, however, concerning the circumstances under which an incompetent person's wishes could be known clearly.

In the majority decision the oral statements which Mrs. O'Connor had made were accorded the status of casual statements which did not constitute "clear and convincing evidence."[26] The court declared that "Nothing less than unequivocal proof will suffice when the decision to terminate life support is at issue.[27] Because Mrs. O'Connor had never given explicit directions concerning artificial nutrition and hydration as such, the court was reluctant to interpret her aversion to artificial means as necessarily indicating an unwillingness to be fed artificially under the present circumstances. The justices who concurred in the majority opinion thought that there was a question as to whether or not Mary O'Connor intended "to choose death by starvation and thirst in her present circumstances."[28] In the absence of an absolutely certain answer to this question, they agreed to err on the side of life.[29]

If Mrs. O'Connor's statements when competent did not give sufficient guidance when she became incompetent, what kind of statements would meet the court's standards? The court majority pointed to statements made by Brother Fox, a member of a religious order, who directed that he be allowed to die if he were ever in a situation like that of Karen Quinlan.[30] Brother Fox's guardian convinced a court that Brother Fox had carefully reflected on the nature of life support which is provided by a respirator, held religious beliefs which allowed for termination of life support, and was mature and serious about the intentions he had expressed. Moreover, Brother Fox's condition and circumstances were identical to Karen Quinlan's, leaving no room for doubt.

The majority also considered a writing, such as a living will, to be a clear expression of a competent person's wishes should he/she become incompetent. It was asserted that a living will would carry more weight than the recounting of casual remarks because

> . . . a person who has troubled to set forth his or her wishes in a writing is more likely than one who has not to make sure that any subsequent changes of heart are adequately expressed, either in a new writing or through clear statements to relatives and friends. In contrast, a person whose expressions of intention were limited to oral statements may not as fully appreciate the need to "rescind" those statements after a change of heart.[31]

The minority was critical of the standards set by the majority for the exercise of the right of self-determination by a once competent patient who becomes incompetent. The minority held that a patient has a right to refuse treatment which will not restore health and that Mrs. O'Connor was entitled to have the court respect and implement her choice not to have "artificial or mechanical support systems."[32] The minority considered Mrs. O'Connor's oral statements consistent, thoughtful and mature and they interpreted them to mean that she did not want to be kept alive by artificial nutrition and hydration.

The minority hypothesized that in the future very few patients will meet the tests for specificity and precision required by the majority,[33] and, as a result, patients' rights to self-determination will not be upheld. Instead of respecting the substituted judgment put forward in good faith by Mrs. O'Connor's daughters, the dissenting justices contended that the majority made its own substituted judgment which it imposed on the patient.[34]

The Barber and Nejdl Case

Clarence Herbert was a 55 year old man who was hospitalized for an ileostomy repair. The surgery was successful but Mr. Herbert suffered a cardio-respiratory arrest while in the recovery room. He was revived and placed on life support equipment. Within a few days it became apparent that Mr. Herbert had sustained severe brain damage which left him in a vegetative state with virtually no hope of recovery. When they were informed of the diagnosis and prognosis Mr. Herbert's wife and children requested "all machines taken off that are sustaining life [sic]."[35] Accordingly, a respirator and other life-sustaining equipment were removed. As it happened, Mr. Herbert was able to breathe on his own. Two days after the removal of the respirator Mr. Herbert's family asked that the intravenous tubes which provided hydration and nourishment be removed. Mr. Herbert's physicians, Neil L. Barber, M.D. and Robert J. Nejdl, M.D., complied with the family's wishes. After cessation of feeding Mr. Herbert was given nursing care which provided for his needs until he died.

Three weeks after Clarence Herbert's death a hospital employee brought the case to the Medico-Legal Office of the District Attorney of Los Angeles. The District Attorney looked into the circumstances of Mr. Herbert's death and charged the physicians who ordered discontinuance of feeding with murder. The Court of Appeal of the State of California entered the case in response to an appeal by the physicians; its task was to determine if the criminal charges approved by the Superior Court of Los Angeles were appropriate. On October 12, 1983 the Court of Appeal of the

State of California handed down a decision stating that the criminal charges should not have been brought and ordered that they be dismissed. The court's decision is especially interesting in respect to its reasoning as to why the physicians should not be charged with murder, its evaluation of the artificial feeding of irreversibly comatose patients, and its assessment of the professional responsibility of physicians who render care to comatose patients. In addition, comments made by the Court of Appeal in regard to the proper domains of the legislature and judiciary are informative.

The Court of Appeal reasoned that Drs. Barber and Nejdl did not commit murder because their participation in the withdrawal of artificial treatment constituted the omission of a form of treatment the physicians had no legal duty to provide. Since "there is no criminal liability to act unless there is a legal duty to act,"[36] the Court concluded that ". . . petitioner's omission to continue treatment under the circumstances, though intentional and with knowledge that the patient would die, was not an unlawful failure to perform a legal duty."[37] Because, according to the California penal code, "murder is the *unlawful* killing of a human being,"[38] and because Drs. Barber and Nejdl did not violate a law and did not take a course construed as being an action (discontinuance of tube feeding being termed an "omission"), there was no legal basis to equate the instruction to stop Mr. Herbert's intravenous feeding as murder.

The Court of Appeal evaluated artificial feeding for irreversibly comatose patients as a medical treatment which may be discontinued. The justices considered artificial procedures for providing nutrition and hydration "more similar to other medical procedures than to typical ways to providing nutrition and hydration."[39] They considered the artificial feeding of a patient such as Clarence Herbert a non-traditional treatment "in that it is not being used to directly cure or even address the pathological condition."[40] When the continued employment of a technique such as artificial feeding is useless, that is, when it does nothing to improve the prognosis for recovery, and when it seems disproportionate, that is, when there appears to be virtually no chance for any significant improvement in condition,[41] the Court of Appeal considered the feeding dispensable. The justices also said that the artificial feeding of comatose patients may be equated with the use of machines such as respirators.[42] In addition, they held that "each drop of fluid produced by intravenous feeding devices is comparable to a manually administered injection or item of medication."[43]

As far as the professional responsibility of physicians who care for comatose patients is concerned, the Court of Appeal cited the standards observed by professionals in one's own locality as the criteria which bind individual practitioners.[44] The court reasoned that physicians do not have a duty to continue treatments which have been proven to be ineffective. It affirmed the ethical principles that physicians should be motivated to serve their patients and should not be prevented from doing so out of a concern for protecting themselves from lawsuits. In this regard the court quoted from the Quinlan decision:

> [T]here must be a way to free physicians in the pursuit of their healing vocation, from possible contamination by self-interest or self-protection concerns which would inhibit their independent medical judgments for the well-being of their dying patients.[45]

The Court of Appeal addressed the fact that there is a significant gap between developments in medical technology and legislation dealing with uses of this technology, leaving physicians and families to make intensely difficult decisions without clear legal guidelines. The court said that an important matter for society to resolve is to determine what is appropriate in the event of "death in which the body lives in some fashion but the brain (or a significant part of it) does not."[46] Once society deals with this question the legislatures of the various states will be able to delineate the specifics of physician responsibility to irreversibly comatose persons.

The court said that the task of deciding how incompetent patients such as Clarence Herbert should be cared for should be determined by the legislature because procedural rules should come from the body most suited for the collection of data and the reaching of a consensus.[47] The court recognized its own responsibility to propose general guidelines and did so by suggesting in what ordinary and extraordinary and proportionate and disproportionate treatment for irreversibly comatose patients might consist. The court also placed decision making for incompetent patients in the hands of their families or guardians and declared that prior judicial approval need not be obtained for decisions entailing withdrawal of treatment.[48]

The Bouvia Case

Elizabeth Bouvia is a woman who was afflicted with cerebral palsy at birth and who, as a result, has virtually no motor function in any of her limbs or other skeletal muscles. She has intact sensory nerves which enable her to experience a fairly constant degree of pain. At the time of her suit against Riverside General Hospital in 1983, Ms. Bouvia was able to eat provided someone was available to feed her. Although she displayed signs of psychological depression,[49] her mind and intelligence were unaffected by her disabilities. Because she was able to understand the benefits and risks attendant to medical procedures to which she could be subject, and because she had the maturity to accept or reject treatments based on her values, Elizabeth Bouvia was considered by the court to be a competent patient.

The action filed by Elizabeth Bouvia while she was a patient at Riverside General Hospital in Riverside, California, asked that the Supreme Court of the State of California for the County of Riverside require that hospital personnel grant her request for pain medication and hygienic care until death occurred, while respecting her refusal to take any nourishment by mouth or by tube. Ms. Bouvia maintained that society had an obligation to assist her in achieving her right to die and she contested the hospital's position that if she remained there she would be fed against her will by "intravenous, nasogastric or gastrostomy tubation."[50]

Officials of Riverside General Hospital argued that allowing a patient who was not terminally ill to starve to death under medical supervision would have "a devastating effect upon the medical staff, administration and patients at Riverside General Hospital; that it would violate medical ethics; that it would constitute participation in the crimes of murder, conspiracy and aiding and abetting suicide; that it would subject the County to civil liability; that it would evoke the wrath of the licensing authority to the hospital, its doctors and its nurses."[51]

The court decided against Elizabeth Bouvia because it reasoned that a severely handicapped, mentally competent person who is not terminally ill does not have the right to be assisted in ending her life. The court asserted that the interests of third parties, including members of the health care professions and other handicapped persons, required it to conclude as it did. The court also directed that if Elizabeth Bouvia continued to receive hospital care, and if she declined to cooperate in being fed, it would be appropriate to force feed her because hospital personnel would have no other reasonable option. Based on the patient's stated intention to die by starvation, her nonterminal physical condition and her life expectancy, the court decided that invasive force feeding would be an ethical course to follow.

In 1986 Elizabeth Bouvia was hospitalized at High Desert Hospital in Los Angeles County. Her condition had worsened from what it was when she was at Riverside General Hospital; the diet and quantity which she was able to consume by mouth was very limited. Ms. Bouvia could orally ingest the soft food which she was spoon fed, but she stopped eating when she felt a tendency to nausea and vomiting, which usually occurred soon after her feeding commenced.[52] Because her weight was very low (in the range of 65 to 70 pounds) the medical staff thought that her oral feedings should be supplemented by nasogastric feedings.[53] Given her unique history, there was an explicit unwillingness on the part of the medical staff to assist Ms. Bouvia should she again be trying to starve herself to death, an intention which she had not declared and which the justices of the Court of Appeal of the State of California, Second Appelate District, did not think was motivating her.[54]

Aware of the concerns of the medical staff Elizabeth Bouvia asked her lawyers to write instructions refusing to allow a feeding tube to be placed in or on her; she signed the instructions by making a feeble "X" on the paper with a pen which she held in her mouth.[55] Even though thus informed of her wishes, the medical staff decided not to honor them. Consequently, Elizabeth Bouvia's oral feedings were supplemented by nasogastric feedings administered against her will.[56] Ms. Bouvia petitioned a trial court to have her NG tube removed. When the trial court denied her request she appealed its decision to the Court of Appeal.

The California Court of Appeal reversed the decision of the trial court and ordered that the nasogastric feeding be discontinued. This decision was based primarily on the fact that competent patients have the right to self-determination. The justices wrote that a competent patient has the right to refuse medical treatment even at risk to hèr health or her very life.[57] In speaking specifically to Elizabeth Bouvia's motives and condition they said:

> As a consequence of her changed condition (since the 1983 court proceedings), it is clear she has now merely resigned herself to accept an earlier death, if necessary, rather than live by feedings forced upon her by means of a nasogastric tube. Her decision to allow nature to take its course is not equivalent to an election to commit suicide with real parties aiding and abetting therein.[58]

In regard to any possible liability of medical personnel who follow directives of competent patients who refuse treatments, the court declared: "No criminal or civil liability attaches to honoring a competent, informed patient's refusal of medical service."[59]

The Cruzan Case

Nancy Cruzan was 24 years old when she was severely injured in an automobile accident on January 11, 1983. As a result of approximately 12-14 minutes of oxygen deprivation, Ms. Cruzan has been comatose ever since. She has been diagnosed as being in a vegetative state with no hope of recovery. Joe and Joyce Cruzan, her parents, were appointed her co-guardians and in 1987 they asked the Jasper County Circuit Court to allow discontinuance of their daughter's feeding by a gastrostomy tube. On July 27, 1988 Judge Charles E. Teel granted their request. Although her guardian *ad litem* believed that it was in Ms. Cruzan's "best interests to have the tube feeding discontinued," he thought that an appeal to the highest court in Missouri was in order "in view of the fact that this is a case of first impression in the State of Missouri."[60] After examining the reasoning on which the judgment of the trial court was based, the Supreme Court of Missouri decided that the lower court had erroneously declared the law and reversed that court's decision.[61]

The Supreme Court of Missouri based its decision that the trial court had erroneously declared the law on the fact that the trial court applied the precedents set in such cases as Brophy, Conroy and Bouvia to the Cruzan case *without determining whether or not these precedents were truly valid.* It was the conclusion of the Missouri Supreme Court that the reasoning in Brophy, Conroy, Bouvia and other similar cases is essentially flawed.

These cases which allowed for discontinuance of artificial feeding took direction from earlier cases such as Quinlan (1976), Saikewicz (1977) and Eichner/Storar (1981). Requests on behalf of three of the four incompetent patients involved in these cases were for discontinuance or non-initiation of treatment for an incompetent *terminally ill* patient. Justices hearing those cases concluded that discontinuing life support or not beginning chemotherapy because of its serious side effects (Saikewicz) allowed patients to die of underlying pathologies. (On the other hand, the request of John Storar's mother that her profoundly retarded 52 year old son who suffered from metastatic cancer not be given blood transfusions was denied because "A court would not allow a parent to deny a child all treatment for a condition which threatens his life."[62])

The Supreme Court of Missouri reasoned that in view of the fact that Claire Conroy, Paul Brophy, and Elizabeth Bouvia were different from Quinlan, Saikewicz, and Brother Fox (the patient in the Eichner case) in that they were not terminally ill, it did not follow on the basis of precedents in the Quinlan/Saikewicz/Eichner-Storar trilogy that the cessations of these patients' treatments were justified. In the same vein the court argued that Nancy Cruzan's artificial feeding should not be discontinued because Ms. Cruzan is not terminally ill and actually has a life expectancy of perhaps thirty years.

The Supreme Court of Missouri rejected the argument that a patient's exercise of the constitutionally guaranteed right of privacy includes the substituted judgment of a surrogate that artificial nutrition and hydration constitute an extreme measure which would not be wanted by the patient. The court stated: "Based on our analysis of the right to privacy decision of the (U.S.) Supreme Court, we carry grave doubts as to the applicability of privacy rights to decisions to terminate the provision of food and water to an incompetent patient."[63] Even if in some cases privacy rights were construed as including the termination of artificial feeding, the justices indicated specific reasons why the request of Mr. and Mrs. Cruzan should not be granted. They cited the fact that Ms. Cruzan was not terminally ill and they contended that the state has an interest in protecting vulnerable incompetents such as Ms. Cruzan. Protecting Ms. Cruzan's life, and not making value judgments regarding the quality of that life, was seen as the proper role of the state. "Were quality of life at issue, persons with all manner of handicaps might find the state seeking to terminate their lives. Instead, the state's interest is in life; that interest is unqualified."[64] Accordingly, the court rejected the argument that Ms. Cruzan had no hope of recovery and thus should be allowed to die because such reasoning "is but a thinly veiled statement that her life in its present form is not worth living."[65] Since it did not consider artificial feeding a burden to Nancy Cruzan[66] and since it thought that it was of vital interest to the state to "err on the side of protecting life,"[67] the Supreme Court of Missouri concluded that there was no "principled legal basis which permits the co-guardians in this case to choose the death of their ward."[68]

Three dissenting opinions were filed which criticized virtually every conclusion reached by the majority as well as the premises on which the conclusions were based. On March 13, 1989, Mr. and Mrs. Cruzan asked the United States Supreme Court to permit doctors to disconnect their daughter's gastrostomy tube. The U.S. Supreme Court has agreed to hear the case; it will be the first time it acts on a case to allow discontinuance of artificial feeding from an incompetent patient. Its decision is expected in 1990.

The Direction of the Courts on Issues Related to Artificial Feeding

The technology for providing artificial nutrition and hydration to severely brain damaged patients came into general use in hospitals and nursing homes before state legislatures had an opportunity to formulate laws to cover instances of forgoing and withdrawing such treatment. Many patients learned about the procedure as they were intubated with pliable silastic tubes which were guided through their noses and down to their stomachs. Patients, next of kin, physicians, nurses and healthcare administrators have dealt with the issues which accompany the technology without having had legal guidelines or systematic ethical reflection available to them. Within this climate courts in the United States have found that they are leading the way in reviewing the legal and ethical aspects of decisions relating to artificial feeding. It is important to understand that decisions made in one state provide guidance but do not settle issues in other jurisdictions. It is also important to realize that within a given jurisdiction the decision of a court is applicable only if a subsequent case is characterized by facts and circumstances which are comparable. At this point in the history of artificial feeding the courts have provided society with direction concerning use and nonuse of the technology. Interest in such highly publicized cases as the ones just reviewed has led to increasing awareness of the radical changes the availability of artificial feeding has brought to the practice of medicine as well as to the possibilities of survival for comatose patients as well as those who are prevented by other maladies from being able to eat and drink. The precedents which have been established together with an increasing level of public awareness is leading to an appreciation of the multifaceted implications of the technology.

Principles articulated by various courts in conjunction with deliberations on cases relating to artificial sustenance provide the rationale for the occasional limitation of their use. As far as competent patients are concerned, these principles are straightforward. Competent persons have a right to exercise self-determination and autonomy in the choice or refusal of treatment; the right to privacy, safeguarded by the United States Constitution, assures protection to those who exercise self-determination in medical matters. Since a competent person, regardless of diagnosis or prognosis, has the right to refuse artificial feeding, health caregivers should honor such wishes unless doing so would be tantamount to assisting in a suicide.

In respect to the interests of the state, the courts delineate these as preventing homicide and suicide, upholding the integrity of the medical profession, and acting to insure the wellbeing of vulnerable persons, such as children and the retarded. When confronted with requests to discontinue the artificial feeding of incompetent patients the courts seek to uphold patient autonomy as well as the interests of the state. Their goal is to achieve a balance and to present their reasons as to why a particular position is balanced in a persuasive way to the communities they serve. In resolving the issue of withdrawal of artificial feeding from incompetent patients four principles seem to be emerging. First, a writing such as a living will which clearly expresses an individual's choices in regard to terminating artificial feeding in circumstances which approximate those which are actually occurring should be honored. Second, patients who have diminished mental functioning, who are ill but not dying, and whose directives about being fed artificially under the specific circumstances in which they find themselves are nonexistent or vague should continue to be tube fed in order to avoid errors of interpretation. Third, tube feeding of incompetent patients who are beyond sentience in a persistent vegetative state and whose oral directives leave little or no room for doubt about their not wanting to be kept alive by artificial means may be withdrawn. Fourth, in regard to incompetent patients who were never competent and who are receiving tube feeding, since their wishes were never made known and since the state has an interest in protecting them, tube feeding should be continued unless it becomes clearly burdensome.

What are the proper domains of the courts and the family when decisions about artificial feeding of incompetent patients need to be resolved? There is a general consensus that the family is the proper locus for decision making. It would be very time-consuming and cumbersome to involve courts routinely in such decisions, but court intervention may become necessary if medical caregivers fear that family members are not motivated by the best interests of the patient, if agreement cannot be reached among the members of a family, or if there are no next of kin.

From their decisions on artificial feeding it appears that the courts understand the responsibilities of health professionals in traditional terms: to do no unnecessary harm, to prescribe treatments which have curative and restorative potential as well as those which will prevent harm or provide comfort, and, in the face of death, to provide for the alleviation of suffering. In addition, the courts acknowledge that physicians act at the behest of the patient and may not render treatment without patient consent.

Doubts of fact continue to exist about two critically important tube feeding issues. First, the nature of tube feeding: Is it nourishment very similar to food and drink taken by mouth or a medical technology which carries attendant risks? Second, how painful or nonpainful is the subjective experience of dying for patients who are capable of some degree of feeling and for whom the cessation of tube feeding is a possibility? These as yet unresolved questions result in an ambiguity in regard to delineating precise judicial guidelines for use and withdrawal of artificial nutrition and hydration from many classes of incompetent patients, especially nonterminally ill incompetents with uncertain advance directives.

Legislative Action: Advance Directives or Living Will Laws

A living will is a statement which is signed and witnessed and which contains instructions for physicians and family members about what treatment is desired by a person should that person become incompetent. The tendency of persons who execute living wills is to give directions regarding withholding or terminating life-prolonging medical procedures when there is virtually no possibility of being restored to health.

As of 1987 living will legislation had been passed by 39 state legislatures. Living will laws vary from state to state but, in general, living will legislation provides:

- recognition of an adult individual's advance directive regarding medical care in the event of a terminal condition.

- immunity from legal liability for medical caregivers who honor directives as required by the statute.

- a suggested form for the declaration, which in most states may be varied with personal directions.

- definitions of the terms of the statute, such as life-sustaining procedure and terminal condition. The definitions vary from state to state, and misunderstandings frequently result from a failure to closely read the statutory language.

- procedures for execution of declarations, such as witnessing requirements, and easily met revocation procedures.

- an unlimited term of effectiveness of the declaration, unless revoked, in every state except California.[69]

In regard to withholding or withdrawing artificial feeding from terminally ill or permanently unconscious patients, 24 of 39 state statutes address this issue. Seven (Colorado, Connecticut, Georgia, Idaho, Maine, Missouri and Wisconsin) say that artificial feeding may not be rejected under the law. Four (Alaska, Arkansas, Montana and Tennessee) indicate that artificial feeding not needed for comfort may be withheld or withdrawn. Thirteen (Arizona, Florida, Hawaii, Illinois, Indiana, Iowa, Maryland, New Hampshire, Oklahoma, South Carolina, Utah, West Virginia and Wyoming) associate tube feeding with comfort care and their statutes are ordinarily interpreted as not allowing for its withholding or withdrawal.[70]

A recent development involved a court test of the Florida living will statute. In 1984 the Florida Life-Prolonging Procedure Act was passed. This act specifically excluded the "provision of sustenance" from its definition of "life-prolonging procedure" which may be the subject of the right to decline.[71] Helen Corbett, a patient in a persistent vegetative state since March 13, 1982, was fed by means of a nasogastric tube beginning in the autumn of 1982. Her husband Thomas E. Corbett wanted the tube removed so that his wife could die. Both the health care providers and the trial court to which Mr. Corbett went refused to grant his request. On April 18, 1986 the district Court of Appeal to which Mr. Corbett appealed the lower court ruling overturned the decision of the first court and concluded that removal of NG feeding was a privacy right which was protected by the United States Constitution. The court reasoned that State laws cannot abrogate the constitutionally guaranteed rights of U. S. citizens, and laws which seem to do so are invalid. The justices held

> . . . although chapter 765, in those cases to which it applies, excludes the right to decline sustenance providing life-prolonging measures, that chapter does not affect the otherwise existing constitutional rights of persons in a permanent vegetative state with no reasonable prospect of regaining cognitive brain function to forego the use of artificial life sustaining means.[72]

Unfortunately, even though Florida has living will legislation, this legislation apparently does not take sufficient account of all the complex aspects of cessation of treatment and may require amendment in order to do so. In light of this possibility, other states which do not allow for forgoing or withdrawing of tube feeding under any circumstances may face court tests similar to the one brought by Thomas Corbett in Florida, and their legislation which was only recently enacted may have to be revised.

Insight Offered by Task Forces and Other Groups

The widespread use of artificial nutrition and hydration has prompted many different groups to speak to issues related to this technology within the context of their values, and to issue policy statements. These statements have in common the facts that they were formulated after serious study, consultation and dialogue, and they are offered to the American public in order to promote understanding of and reflection upon various points of view. A review of some of the position papers which have been released provides insight and may also alert us to cautions which ought to be observed.

The members of the President's Commission for the Study of Ethical Problems in Medicine and Biomedical and Behavioral Research worked for three years before unanimously issuing a report of more than 500 pages on December 15, 1982. Because "matters once the province of fate have now become a matter of human choice, a development that has profound ethical and legal implications," the Commission undertook the task of trying to clarify the issues surrounding deciding to forgo the wide range of life-sustaining treatments available today, including artificial nutrition and hydration.[73] Its advice to state courts and legislatures to make provisions for advance directives, (living wills) and durable power of attorney statutes (documents which provide for the appointment of an agent for medical decision making if a patient becomes incapacitated) is, by and large, being heeded. The Commission affirmed the traditional model for medical decision making, valuing the special competence of the physician in regard to diagnosis and treatment options, and upholding the autonomy of competent patients. In cases involving incompetent patients, the Commission considered the patient's family and friends the persons best suited to choose from among the available options. An apt summary of the Commission's consensus states:

> . . . the Commission finds good decisionmaking regarding patients who have permanently lost consciousness to be possible without changes in law or other public policy. The medical profession should continue to carry its weighty obligation to establish diagnoses well and to help families understand these tragic situations. Health care institutions need to provide good policies to govern

decision making, including appropriate sources of consultation and advice. Family and friends of the permanently unconscious patient bear not only the protracted tragedy of their loss but also the substantial responsibility of collaborating in decision making. When families can direct the care of an unconscious family member, practices and policies should encourage them to do so—and should restrict the degree to which outsiders may intervene in these matters. Courts and legislatures should not encourage routine resort to the judicial system for the actual decision making. Instead, courts ought to ensure that appropriate surrogates are designated and that surrogates are allowed an appropriate range of discretion.[74]

The New Jersey Commission on Legal and Ethical Problems in the Delivery of Health Care was established by the state legislature as a permanent commission of 27 members on November 12, 1985. On June 8, 1988 the Commission adopted three principles pertaining to the artificial provision of fluids and nutrition. Three conclusions are expressed in these principles. First, tube feeding is a medical treatment and should not be characterized as outside the scope of medical treatments. Second, either compelling tube feeding or prohibiting its withdrawal without regard to the facts of individual cases are not legally or ethically justified. And third, the state should establish safeguards to protect vulnerable patients for whom the forgoing or withdrawal of tube feeding is a possibility because in so doing it upholds the important social value of public confidence in the caring role of medical professionals.

The Council on Ethical and Judicial Affairs of the American Medical Association presented its position on forgoing and withdrawing tube feeding in March, 1986. The AMA went on record as evaluating artificially supplied nutrition and hydration as a medical treatment which is appropriately placed in the same category as a respirator. It also stated that it is not unethical to cease tube feeding of patients who are in a persistent vegetative state, even if death is not imminent. For patients who are not in a persistent vegetative state and who have not issued oral or written advance directives, the AMA seems to favor initiation and continuation of artificial feeding:

Unless it is clearly established that the patient is terminally ill or irreversibly comatose, a physician should not be deterred from appropriately aggressive treatment of a patient.[75]

On April 10, 1986 the United Handicapped Federation of the State of Minnesota, an organization of 28 groups with approximately 12,000 members, approved a series of resolutions dealing with artificial nutrition and hydration. The Federation acted out of a concern that future focus on cost containment might lead to public policy decisions authorizing nontreatment for broader categories of disabled persons than only patients who are in a persistent vegetative state. The consensus which emerged from the Federation was that

... full access to nutrition and hydration, and to ordinary medical treatment, including antibiotics, whether administered by usual physical means or by artificial or technological assistance, to be a basic right of all persons, regardless of age, whether or not they have disabilities, and whether or not they are terminally ill.[76]

The UHF did not address difficult cases involving how to determine an incompetent patient's wishes or best interests so as to act in conformity to them; the special interests of its membership lie elsewhere. It is precisely these special interests which alert society to the danger of sliding down a slippery slope by any decisions which could be construed as compromising a belief in the dignity of each and every person which the UHF sought to emphasize. Cautions advocated by organizations such as the UHF are considered by state courts and legislatures when these bodies deal with issues related to artificial feeding and hydration.

Guidelines on the termination of life-sustaining treatment formulated by the Hastings Center, a private research group which analyzes issues in biomedical ethics and is located in Briarcliff Manor, N.Y., include recommendations regarding artificial nutrition and hydration.[77] One recommendation is especially interesting in that, if it is adopted, it would change the procedures followed prior to nonsurgical tube feeding:

All invasive procedures for supplying nutrition and hydration—all enteral and parenteral techniques—should be considered procedures that the patient or surrogate may choose to forgo. This includes not only procedures such as use of a gastrostomy or jejunostomy tube, but also the nasogastric (NG) tube and the peripheral intravenous line (IV). The practice has been not to seek consent for these latter two procedures because they have been considered part of the routine care consented to on admission to the healthcare institution. However, all medical techniques for supplying nutrition and hydration should be a matter of choice by the patient or surrogate, except when begun on an emergency basis with no time for consent. . .[78]

If this recommendation were to become standard hospital policy, then recourse to the courts in situations similar to Claire Conroy's would not be necessary. I base this conclusion on the fact that Thomas Whittemore said that, if consulted, he would not have consented to his aunt's being fed by an NG tube. In emergency cases such as those of Paul Brophy and Nancy Cruzan wherein the recovery hoped for at the outset eventually became an impossible goal, such a policy would not have eliminated the controversy surrounding requests to discontinue feeding. While the Hastings Center guidelines do not refer to specific cases or circumstances (e.g., patients in a persistent vegetative state) as indicative of reasonable grounds for withdrawing artificial nutrition and hydration, they do state that it is ethical to withdraw artificial feeding if "the life these procedures offer may impose burdens that exceed their benefit to the patient, or may be contrary to the patient's wishes."[79]

On November 10, 1984, the Committee for Pro-Life Activities of the National Conference of Catholic Bishops issued "Guidelines for Legislation on Life-Sustaining Treatment." The ten recommendations which they propose are as follows:

(a) Presuppose the fundamental right to life of every human being, including the disabled, the elderly and the terminally ill. In general, phrases which seem to romanticize death, such as "right to die" or "death with dignity," should be avoided.

(b) Recognize that the right to refuse medical treatment is not an independent right, but is a corollary to the patient's right and moral responsibility to request reasonable treatment. The law should demonstrate no preference for protecting only the right to *refuse* treatment, particularly when *life-sustaining* treatment is under consideration.

(c) Place the patient's right to determine medical care within the context of other factors which limit the exercise of that right— e.g., the state's interest in protecting innocent third parties, preventing homicide and suicide, and maintaining good ethical standards in the healthcare profession. Policy statements which define the right to refuse treatment in terms of the patient's constitutional rights (e.g., a "right of privacy") tend to inhibit the careful balancing of all the interests that should be considered in such cases.

(d) Promote communication among patient, family and physician. Current "living will" laws tend to have the opposite effect—that of excluding family members and other loved ones from the decision-making process. As a general rule, documents and legal proceedings are no substitute for a physician's personal consultation with the patient and/or family at the time a decision must be made on a particular course of treatment.

(e) Avoid granting unlimited power to a document or proxy decision-maker to make healthcare decisions on a patient's behalf. The right to make such decisions on one's own behalf is itself not absolute, and in any event cannot be fully exercised when a patient has had no opportunity to assess the burdens and benefits of treatment in a specific situation. Laws which allow a decision to be made on behalf of a mentally incompetent patient must include safeguards, to insure that the decision adequately represents the patient's wishes or best interests and is in accord with responsible medical practice.

(f) Clarify the rights and responsibilities of physicians without granting blanket immunity from all legal liability. No physician should be protected from liability for acting homicidally or negligently. Nor should new legal penalties be imposed on a physician for failing to obey a patient's or proxy's wishes when such obedience would violate the physician's ethical convictions or professional standards.

(g) Reaffirm public policies against homicide and assisted suicide. Medical treatment legislation may clarify procedures for discontinuing treatment which only secures a precarious and burdensome prolongation of life for the terminally ill patient, but should not condone or authorize any deliberate act or omission designed to cause a patient's death.

(h) Recognize the presumption that certain basic measures such as nursing care, hydration, nourishment, and the like must be maintained out of respect for the human dignity of every patient.

(i) Protect the interests of innocent parties who are not competent to make treatment decisions on their own behalf. Life-sustaining treatment should not be discriminatorily withheld or withdrawn from mentally incompetent or retarded patients.

(j) Provide that life-sustaining treatment should not be withdrawn from a pregnant woman if continued treatment may benefit her unborn child.

In these guidelines, the hierarchical leadership of the Catholic Church in the United States seeks to communicate principles enshrined in Catholic medical ethics. In so doing the NCCB makes explicit the insight and wisdom of the Catholic tradition to members of the Church and offers them to the broader society for consideration. This insight includes an understanding of persons as individuals who have responsibility to take reasonable care of their health and to contribute their unique gifts to the human community. By suggesting that rights are accompanied by responsibilities, the bishops hope to correct an overly individualistic concept of patients' rights.

Fearing the possibility that incompetents might be abused by those who should protect their best interests, the NCCB urges that the state fulfill its function of protecting vulnerable persons who are in jeopardy. In addition, the bishops emphasize a strong bias for life and a total unwillingness to move in the direction of permitting legal sanction for suicide or direct euthanasia. They state a presupposition in favor of providing certain basic measures such as nursing care, hydration, nutrition and the like "out of respect for the human dignity of patients." (It is my opinion that the

NCCB would not mandate artificial feeding of a patient if such treatment were a burden because, in such circumstances, artificial feeding would detract from the patient's dignity.) To the extent that forgoing or withdrawing artificial nutrition and hydration constitutes denying patients appropriate care, the NCCB emphatically rejects such a denial as contrary to its principles.

Conclusion

The technology of artificial feeding ordinarily enhances patient care and provides benefits. Instances in which surrogates request the discontinuance of tube feeding from incompetents have proved very perplexing. In the absence of legislation specifying courses of action which may or may not be taken in particular circumstances, U.S. courts have been called upon to endorse or reject requests for cessation of artificial feeding. By far the most difficult cases to decide have involved surrogate requests for discontinuance of tube feeding made on behalf of incompetents who did not leave clear advance directives and who are not terminally ill.

Special interest groups which have offered input in the hope of affecting public policy with regard to use and nonuse of artificial nutrition and hydration have performed a public service by articulating the values and philosophy which they seek to promote. Continued discussion and clarification is desirable in order to move beyond confusion and ambiguity. Given the widespread contemporary availability of the technology, there is no question of the need to reach consensus on when artificial feeding can be forgone or withdrawn. Reaching such a consensus is a prerequisite to enacting appropriate legislation and disengaging the courts from the process of medical decision making.

Endnotes

1. Brophy v. New England Sinai Hospital, Inc., Mass. Probate County Ct., Norfolk Division, (No. 85E0009-G1.), October 21, 1985, p. 9.

2. Ibid.

3. Ibid., p. 21.

4. Ibid., pp. 42, 43.

5. Ibid., p. 42.

6. Brophy v. New England Sinai Hospital, Inc., 497 N.E. 2d 626 (Mass. 1986).

7. In re Conroy 98 NJ 321, 486 A. 2d (1985), p. 1209.

8. Ibid., p. 1218.

9. Ibid., p. 1209.

10. Ibid., p. 1218.

11. Ibid., p. 1232.

12. Ibid., p. 1230.

13. Ibid., p. 1231.

14. Ibid., p. 1232.

15. Ibid., p. 1233.

16. In the Matter of Mary O'Connor, 2 NY 2d 312, p. 4.

17. Ibid., p. 5.

18. Ibid.

19. Ibid., p. 6.

20. Ibid., p. 20.

21. Ibid., p. 19.

22. M/0 Westchester County Medical Center v. Hall, No. 312-RDS, p. 7.

23. Ibid.

24. Ibid., p. 10.

25. Ibid.

26. Op.cit., the Matter of Mary O'Connor, p. 18.

27. Ibid., p. 13.

28. Ibid., p. 21.

29. Ibid., p. 15.

30. Ibid., p. 13; cf., Matter of Storar and Matter of Eichner, 52 NY 2nd 363.

31. Ibid., p. 16.

32. Op.cit., M/O, p. 16.

33. Ibid., p. 16.

34. Ibid., p. 21.

35. Barber v. Superior Court, 147 Cal. App. 3d 1006 (1983), p. 3.

36. Ibid., p. 15.

37. Ibid., p. 24.

38. Ibid., p. 4.

39. Ibid., p. 14.

40. Ibid., p. 15.

41. Ibid., p. 18.

42. Ibid., p. 13.

43. Ibid.

44. Ibid., p. 15.

45. Ibid., p. 17; section quoted is from Matter of Quinlan (1976) 355 A. 2d 647, at p. 668.

46. Ibid., p. 9; quoted from Severns v. Wilmington Medical Center, Inc. (1980) 421 A2d. 1334, 1344.

47. Ibid., p. 17.

48. Ibid., p. 23.

49. Bouvia v. County of Riverside, No. 159780 (Cal. Super. Ct. Riverside County, Dec. 16, 1983) (Hews, J.), p. 5.

50. Ibid., p. 1.

51. Ibid., p. 2.

52. Bouvia v. Superior Court (Glenchur), 2nd Civ. No. B019134 (Super. Ct. No. C583828), Apr. 16, 1986, p. 7.

53. Ibid.

54. Ibid., pp. 7, 24.

55. Ibid., p. 7.

56. Ibid., pp. 2, 7.

57. Ibid., p. 12.

58. Ibid., p. 24.

59. Ibid., p. 25.

60. Cruzan v. Harmon v. McCanse, Supreme Court of Missouri, No. 70813, Nov. 16, 1988, p. 2.

61. Ibid.

62. Ibid., p. 12.

63. Ibid., p. 22.

64. Ibid., p. 27.

65. Ibid., p. 32.

66. Ibid., p. 35.

67. Ibid., p. 41.

68. Ibid., p. 43.

69. Society for the Right to Die, *Handbook of Living Will Laws*, 1987 Edition (New York: The Society for the Right to Die, 1987), p. 15.

70. Ibid., pp. 6,7.

71. Florida Life-Prolonging Procedure Act 1984, Fla. Stat. Ann. 765.03 (3) (b).

72. Corbett v. D'Alessandro, 487 So. 2d 368 (Fla. Dist. Ct. App.) 1986 P. 5.

73. President's Commission for the Study of Ethical Problems in Medicine and Biomedical and Behavioral Research, *Deciding to Forego Life-Sustaining Treatment* (Washington, DC: U. S. Government Printing Office, 1983), pp. 1, 2.

74. Ibid., p. 196.

75. Current Opinions of the Council on Ethical and Judicial Affairs of the American Medical Association, 1986, par. 2.19.

76. Press Release, The United Handicapped Federation and the Friends of Handicapped People Association, St. Paul, MN, April 10, 1986.

77. The Hastings Center, *Guidelines on the Termination of Life-Sustaining Treatment and the Care of the Dying* (Bloomington, IN: Indiana University Press, 1987), pp. 59-62.

78. Ibid., p. 61.

79. Ibid., p. 60.

3

Moral Considerations in Regard to Decision Making

Introduction

Morality is concerned with developing principles to guide human conduct as well as practical advice for persons who occasionally have to make complex decisions involving profound human goods. The most basic moral postulate is "Do good and avoid evil." Because there is a presumption in favor of sustaining life, legislators, hospital administrators and healthcare professionals are likely to equate the maintenance of life with the good which they are ethically required to do. The force of this obligation is ordinarily self-evident. Occasionally it happens, however, that technology dehumanizes the process of dying and causes discomfort and pain, or maintains a vegetative existence which runs counter to a patient's advance directive or the best interests of the patient as understood by next of kin. Under such circumstances it is imperative to determine whether the perceived responsibility of those who are inclined to prescribe such treatments as tube feeding is correct, or if there are reasonable moral grounds to omit/remove feeding tubes. Arriving at moral judgments of this type requires an ability to make critically important distinctions within the framework of a clearly-delineated ethical system. In this chapter we will consider the context in which tube feeding decisions are made and some norms and distinctions which provide guidance for moral decision makers as well as the state of the question within Catholic moral theology.

The Context within which Decisions Are Made

In a speech at Loyola University of Chicago on May 8, 1985, Joseph Cardinal Bernardin, archbishop of Chicago, spoke of the importance of

57

one's attitude toward life as of fundamental significance in approaching the issues of modern times which threaten life:

> The pre-condition for sustaining a consistent ethic is a "respect life" attitude or atmoshpere in society. Where human life is considered "cheap" and easily "wasted," eventually nothing is held as sacred and all lives are in jeopardy . . . The purpose of proposing a consistent ethic of life is to argue that success on any one of the issues threatening life requires a concern for the broader attitude in society about respect for life. Attitude is the place to root an ethic of life.[1]

In the United States today human life is threatened by forces as diverse as poverty, nuclear weapons, illegal drugs and wanton criminal acts. Human life is quietly snuffed out by abortion and sometimes sensationally terminated at well-publicized executions of criminals. Disrespect for human life tends to foster a general malaise which is frequently accompanied by confusion regarding the sacred value of each individual life. Fostering an attitude of reverence for individual persons as well as respect for all of God's creation is a prerequisite for developing a sound ethical vision within which to consider issues involving life and death. A reverent attitude toward life can seem counter-cultural. Bearers of such an attitude frequently find themselves having to defend their positions against arguments from advocates for such causes as pro-choice on abortion, capital punishment and euthanasia. Understanding why one holds a consistent ethic of life, and committing oneself to make choices consistent with such a moral vision requires comprehension of the cultural context in which life-related issues are made as well as the inherent reasonableness of the principles to which one adheres. In regard to questions of use, nonuse and discontinuance of artificial nutrition and hydration, a clear grasp of the ethical aspects of decision making is absolutely essential.

The cultural context in which life-related issues such as those concerned with artificial sustenance are resolved is a complex reality which includes two widely divergent viewpoints. The first can be characterized as a vitalist mentality; its opposite consists in the advocacy of euthanasia. In a medical context vitalism refers to the conviction that any/all life-sustaining measures should be employed in the treatment of a sick or dying person, with the moment of death stalled as long as humanly possible. For the vitalist, decision making is fairly straightforward: the use of each and every available routine and experimental therapy is endorsed. Accordingly, it would be unlikely for vitalists to reject the initiation or continuation of artificial feeding except in cases in which tube feeding is clearly contraindicated on medical grounds.

Advocacy of euthanasia represents the extreme opposite of a vitalist mentality. The word euthanasia is made up of two Greek words, *eu* and *thanatos* and means "a good death." The sense which the adjective "good" originally conveyed was painless or easy. The predominant way in which the concept of euthanasia is understood today is that euthanasia consists in the taking of specific actions to bring about death, either on the part of patients themselves or on the part of their agents. Even though it is illegal, there seems to be increasing acceptance of the idea of practicing euthanasia in contemporary society when this is in accord with a patient's wish. A patient can effect euthanasia by taking an overdose of barbiturates; a patient's relative or friend can effect euthanasia by a variety of means. Scenarios are even suggested within which physicians or nurses practice euthanasia but there is no evidence that healthcare workers have any interest in doing so. Proponents of euthanasia justify it because they see it as bringing an end to pain and suffering. Slogans such as "death with dignity" and the "right to die" appear regularly in the polemic of advocates of euthanasia. In regard to tube feeding of patients who are terminally ill, elderly and demented, or irreversibly comatose, persons who favor euthanasia would probably deny the existence of any interest the state might claim in requiring tube feeding under particular circumstances or any sense of moral responsibility a patient or guardian might experience to preserve life in a diminished condition. It is difficult to estimate the strength of the present day euthanasia movement in the United States; within the perspective of a consistent ethic of life, however, this movement is evaluated as fundamentally disrespectful toward life.

The Roman Catholic medical-ethical tradition is obviously at variance with a euthanasiast mentality. The Catholic tradition adheres to the belief that life is God's good gift and that, to honor God's gift, people should respect their embodied existence and take care of their health. Even though contemporary men and women who are terminally ill are able to exercise many options in regard to medications and therapies, and can, by so-doing, hasten or stall death, an implicit religious conviction remains that at a given time God causes the transformation of each mortal life into a new mode of existence. This belief, along with moral analysis of proper and improper forms of human conduct, has resulted in an absolute prohibition of overt actions which result in the death of a sick or dying person. The responsibility of family members, friends and medical professionals is understood in terms of rendering care to the ill and dying and keeping company with them. A proper response consists in offering appropriate treatments and alleviating physical pain and emotional distress by employing palliative measures and extending sympathy, support and encouragement.

The Catholic medical-ethical tradition is also at odds with a vitalist mentality. Vitalists and Catholic Christians disagree in their assessments of death. Vitalists tend to think of death in the most negative of terms and want to do everything possible to prevent it. Fear of death along with absence of belief in an afterlife may provide the motivation for adopting a vitalist attitude. Catholics, on the other hand, have learned to think of death as an event which changes life but does not take it away. Catholics are apt to think that it is right for nature to take its course because they believe that suffering and death are a prelude to a person's entering into the fullness of life. Allowing death to claim a dying or terminally ill person by not employing every available medical treatment is an acceptable moral option within the Catholic medical-ethical tradition. Indeed, this is the essence of the hospice philosophy which holds so much appeal to Catholic Christians and many other members of society as well. (The hospice movement aims to assist the terminally ill and dying by providing emotional and spiritual support and palliative care in a home or home-like setting; it provides terminally ill patients and their next of kin with an alternative to the routine and procedures of the hospital.)

The Roman Catholic medical-ethical tradition has always expressed reverence for embodied existence, the continuum extending from conception until natural death, during which persons live out their individual lives. Catholic teaching has held that people should take reasonable care of their health. The Church's assessment of biological life is that it is a great good but not an absolute good. (God alone is the absolute good.) Because life is not an absolute good, it is not necessary to employ every available therapy so as to live as long as medical science makes possible. Physical life is not the only value people hold; they also value comfort, the company of loved ones, familiar surroundings and the peace of mind of knowing that they have sufficient funds to provide for dependents after they die. In recognizing these and other values the Church has offered the instruction that people should use *ordinary means* to take care of their health, but that they are not morally obliged to use *extraordinary means*.

The late Gerald Kelly, S.J., a respected moral theologian, provided definitions for ordinary and extraordinary means of preserving life as these terms are commonly used by theologians:

> Ordinary means of preserving life are all medicines, treatments, and operations which offer a reasonable hope of benefit for the patient and/or which can be obtained and used without excessive expense, pain or other inconvenience; extraordinary means are all medicines, treatments, and operations, which cannot be obtained or used without excessive expense, pain, or other inconvenience.[2]

In 1957 Pope Pius XII provided an explanation of why the Church teaches that it is only ordinary means which are required:

> . . . normally, one is held to use only ordinary means—according to the circumstances of persons, places, times and cultures—that is to say, means that do not involve any grave burden for oneself or another. A more strict obligation would be too burdensome for most men and would render the attainment of a higher, more important good too difficult. Life, health, all temporal activities are in fact subordinated to spiritual ends. On the other hand, one is not forbidden to take more than the strictly necessary steps to preserve life and health, as long as he does not fail in some serious duty.[3]

The 1980 *Declaration on Euthanasia*, issued by the Sacred Congregation for the Doctrine of the Faith (an office of the Vatican), said that the statement that "one is never obliged to use 'extraordinary' means" still holds good, but may be "less clear today by reason of the imprecision of the term and the rapid progress made in the treatment of sickness."[4] Accordingly, the Vatican document cited the preference of some people to speak of " 'proportionate' and 'disproportionate' means." "In any case," the Declaration continued, "it will be possible to make a correct judgment as to means by studying the type of treatment to be used, its degree of complexity or risk, its cost and the possibilities of using it, and comparing these elements with the result that can be expected, taking into account the state of the sick person and his or her physical and moral resources."[5] If the benefits of the proposed treatment would probably outweigh the burdens, then the treatment would be assessed as proportionate; on the other hand, if the burdens of the proposed treatment would probably outweigh the benefits, it would be assessed as disproportionate.

In order to determine what is to count as an ordinary or extraordinary means or which medical course would be proportionate or disproportionate, one would have to know an individual's diagnosis and prognosis and also be familiar with the values the patient holds. The subjective aspect of decision making, i.e., the conviction that it is appropriate for nature to take its course or the desire that the dying process be more or less affected by medical technology emanates from the life experiences and peculiar likes/dislikes of unique individuals. The Catholic Church has consistently respected the right of people "to die peacefully with human and Christian dignity,"[6] and to decide for themselves in what a "dignified death" consists. In the *Declaration on Euthanasia* the Church also reiterated the point made by Pius XII that one may go beyond strictly necessary steps to protect life so that patients may also choose "to have recourse to the means provided by the most advanced medical techniques, even if these are still at the experimental stage and are not without a certain risk."[7]

Through its definitions of ordinary and extraordinary means and its explanation of how a medical course could be proportionate or disproportionate, the Church has provided a framework within which people can make calculations about treatment and has provided the practical common sense guidance that futile, useless, or scarcely beneficial treatments need not be employed. The Church's teaching also allows people to reject treatments which are too expensive or burdensome. (In regard to treatments that are painful, if pain is endured during a treatment course which will very likely end in recovery, it should be endured. If, on the other hand, a painful treatment is offered which holds little promise of leading to recovery, it need not be endured.) While the guidance which the Church offers to people who have to make decisions about medical treaments is helpful, it should be noted that the burden of making calculations and decisions must still be borne by individuals who have to contend with the physical and emotional, as well as the moral aspects of treatment deci-sions.

As difficult as it sometimes is to make reasonable treatment decisions for onself, the situation is much more complicated when family members are called upon to make substituted judgments for incompetent relatives who have not formulated explicit directions regarding their preferences for treatment/nontreatment should they become incompetent. (By substituted judgment is meant the exercise of a patient's right to self-determination by a surrogate who is familiar with the patient's values and wishes and who is recognized legally as the person responsible for decision making. In some cases the surrogate will direct medical practitioners to provide treatment to an incompetent patient; in other cases the surrogate will instruct medical personnel to let a patient die of natural causes without medical intervention. In either instance the substituted judgment of what a patient would want if he or she were competent is made by a person who knows the patient's preferences; a substituted judgment is ethical if it conforms to objective moral norms. The obligation of a surrogate to make a substituted judgment is rooted in the nature of kinship or friendship; the special relationship which binds a relative or friend to an incompetent requires honoring the patient's morally reasonable wishes if the patient is unable to speak for himself or herself.)

Although, the teaching of the Church that persons are free to use their discretion in following objective norms provides Catholics and other inter-ested members of society with a sound and moderate approach to decision making about matters pertaining to health and sickness, it does not remove the sadness and awesome feeling of responsibility experienced by surrogate decision makers who reject extraordinary or disproportionate treatments in order to allow loved ones to die of underlying pathologies.

Norms for Decision Making

During the course of a lifetime people make many important, significant moral decisions. Each time a person has to make a weighty moral decision, he/she becomes aware that something which is of value is on the line. How can that value be upheld? Is upholding the value worth the price that has to be paid? In answering these questions people are acutely aware of their ability to reason and the deeply rooted desire to maintain their integrity. They are also inclined to reach beyond themselves and consult the wisdom offered by church and society. This wisdom is expressed in many forms; one form is that of norms which give direction. Norms are standards which we should follow or rules which establish specific guidelines. In most cases, knowing medical-moral norms is instructive in a general way; however, this knowledge does not eliminate the need to engage in a process of discernment in order to determine the specific course which should be followed in the unique circumstances of particular cases.

When people are making medical decisions for themselves, the following norms are consistent with the Catholic medical-moral tradition:

• Since good health is desirable, reasonable care should be taken to promote it.

• Since illness prevents persons from fulfilling their responsibilities, remedies should be taken in order to bring about the restoration of health.

• Persons with chronic diseases should take such measures as are reasonable to bring about the amelioration of symptoms and the ability to carry out their duties.

• Since persons are bound not to directly attack innocent life, if sick, dying, depressed or otherwise burdened by living, they should not take their own lives by acts of suicide or euthanasia.

• Persons with terminal illnesses should discuss with their physicians all the options which are available to them; they should choose treatments which offer a reasonable hope of benefit and which are not unduly expensive, painful or burdensome. As the disease progresses, they have the right to revise their treatment plan, adding or eliminating therapies according to their best judgment. Their decisions should reflect regard for their total human good, and that of others, so that disease management occurs within this overall context.[8]

It is easier to make a decision for oneself than to do so for another person. There is a much greater tendency to second-guess when making a decision for someone else. In spite of a degree of ambivalence which may be experienced, the following norms provide direction to persons who must make medical decisions for relatives or friends:

• The expressed wishes of an incompetent patient should be honored to the extent possible.

• If the expressed wishes of an incompetent patient were to require a surrogate to perform an overt act of euthanasia or assistance in suicide, these wishes should not be honored.

• In the event that an incompetent patient has not expressed his/her preferences regarding medical treatment, a surrogate decision maker should act in such a way as to protect the patient's best interests.

• A surrogate decision maker should never make a decision for an incompetent patient based upon expedience or self-interest, or with an intent to harm the incompetent.

Members of the medical profession, too, seek to observe objective norms as they serve their patients. These norms include:

• Do no avoidable harm to any patient.

• Do not break the confidence which exists between physician or nurse and patient.

• Provide appropriate remedies for patients who are sick.

• Provide palliative care for patients for whom no remedies are possible.

Of the thirteen norms just suggested, eight are expressed in affirmative terms and five in negative terms. The five negative norms are "Since persons are bound not to directly attack innocent life, . . . they should not take their own lives by acts of suicide or euthanasia," nor should surrogates perform acts of euthanasia or assistance in suicide. "A surrogate decision maker should never make a decision for an incompetent patient based upon expedience or self-interest, or with an intent to harm the incompetent." Members of the medical profession should "Do no avoidable harm to any patient," and they should "not break the confidence which exists between physician or nurse and patient." These negative duties require constant fulfillment at all times; in other words, one must never be doing the thing which is forbidden. In regard to the eight norms which are stated in affirmative terms, however, it is understood that excessive hardship might excuse one from carrying out health-related duties (as the rationale behind the ordinary-extraordinary and proportionate-disproportionate distinctions suggests). In addition, norms expressed in an affirmative fashion imply that people are free to use discretion in regard to when and how they exercise their responsibilities. For example, one parent might postpone making decisions about a child's treatment until such time as the other parent returns home from a business trip, or a physician might wait to prescribe pain medication for a dying patient until the patient's feelings and responses in an unmedicated state are observed.

In regard to nutrition and hydration which are provided artificially via plastic tubes, it needs to be determined how much leeway exists for decision makers who are guided by such moral norms as the ones we just considered. When the issue of use or nonuse of artificial feeding is resolved by a competent patient, that patient has a moral right to make and follow a moral judgment in regard to a treatment course which appears ethically reasonable, or, to put it another way, which is not contrary to moral law. Should the patient opt to be fed artificially, he/she retains the right to discontinue the tube feeding if and when it becomes too expensive, painful or burdensome. The decisions of competent patients are respected by society, the medical profession and the courts because the right of a person to form and follow conscience is inviolable. The specific decisions of conscience which an individual makes cannot help but reflect that person's unique hopes and dreams, values and distastes. The Roman Catholic medical-ethical tradition has exhibited much wisdom in the deference it has afforded to competent individuals who must struggle to make sound and sensible decisions in situations which are growing more and more complicated.

Questions concerning use or nonuse of artificial nutrition and hydration which are most difficult to resolve concern patients who are incompetent. Some incompetent patients provide next of kin with advance directives, but most do not. While advance directives can be very helpful, they frequently contain loopholes. For example, should the wishes of a patient who, when competent, expressed a strong aversion to hospitals and/or sophisticated medical life-support technology, and who stated a desire not to be kept alive on a respirator, be understood, by extrapolation, as including an implicit rejection of tube feeding? Even if a written advance directive includes specific instructions regarding tube feeding, questions can arise as to whether or not the incompetent patient had a change of heart after formulating the document.

Incompetent patients who have given no verbal or written instructions to loved ones present the most difficult cases. Patients who experience a degree of sentience but who are severely demented as well as patients who are irreversibly comatose are candidates for tube feeding. Surrogates who make decisions on behalf of such patients sometimes reject artificial nutrition and hydration because it does (or will) bother, aggravate or irritate the patient, because it offers no hope of benefit, i.e. with or without the treatment the patient will not return to health, or because of a belief that the time of death is at hand and should not be stalled. Next of kin are also likely to argue that, if competent, the patient would prefer to die rather than to live in an "undignified" manner while being artificially fed. (Defining what is "undignified" is necessarily subjective; in addition to the rigorous attention Catholic morality has given to the formulation of objective moral norms, it has also exhibited profound respect for the insights and values of individual decision makers, the so-called subjective element.) In other cases a relative might admit to not knowing what the patient would want, but might judge that, given the circumstances, tube feeding should not be initiated or continued. In these cases there is no doubt that it is the surrogate's convictions which are argued because the patient's are unknown. Provided that the norm "A surrogate decision maker should never make a decision for an incompetent patient based upon expedience or self-interest, or with an intent to harm the incompetent," is not violated, and as long as acts of euthanasia and assistance in suicide are rejected, it is possible that surrogate decision makers are acting ethically and reasonably in not authorizing the initiation of tube feeding or in asking for its discontinuance. This is not to say that they *are acting ethically and reasonably*, only that they *may be* because, while the specifics of a negative duty can be expressed in absolute negative terms, the fulfilling of affirmative obligations requires the use of prudence and discernment and allows for different courses of action depending on the circumstances in individual cases. Cases in which surrogates make decisions for incompetents are not commonplace, but they are growing in frequency partly because of increased longevity with the accompanying physical and mental derioration which sometimes accompany aging.

Roman Catholic Moral Reflection on Forgoing and Withdrawing Artificial Nutrition and Hydration

As we noted in Chapter 2, in the United States some courts have rejected arguments made by sincere and conscientious next of kin, and refused to agree to discontinuance of tube feeding. A question naturally arises as to what direction the Catholic medical-ethical tradition with its well established guidelines offers in these most difficult cases.

Thomas A. Shannon, Professor of Religion and Social Ethics at Worcester Polytechnic Institute, and James J. Walter, Professor of Christian Ethics at Loyola University of Chicago, authored an article entitled "The PVS Patient and the Forgoing/Withdrawing of Medical Nutrition and Hydration," which appeared in the December, 1988 issue of *Theological Studies*. One of the features of this article was a report on a survey of U.S. Catholic dioceses regarding the issue of forgoing and withdrawing artificial feeding from patients in a persistent vegetative state. Some dioceses (a minority of the 167 in the United States) have functioning bioethics committees. Those which did answered a question about whether or not the committee "considered feeding tubes to be a medical technology." "Six said yes; 4 said no; 8 gave no answer, and 1 said 'it depends.' "[9] The authors continue:

The next question was whether the removal of a feeding tube from a PVS patient was ordinary or extraordinary, or if they had no position. Four responded that the care was ordinary, 4 that it was extraordinary, 1 had no position, 9 gave no answer, and 9 said "it depends." The final question asked whether removal was an act of involuntary euthanasia which is direct and forbidden, or indirect and permitted, or no position. Four responded that removal was direct, 5 that it was indirect, 2 had no position, 4 said "it depends," and 8 had no answer.[10]

This survey establishes the fact that at the time it was taken there was a difference of opinion among the diocesan bioethics committees which answered the Shannon-Walter questionnaire regarding the moral evaluation of forgoing and withdrawing artificial feeding from patients in a persistent vegetative state. Differing opinions about this issue have also been expressed by moral theologians, causing confusion for people who consult these authorities for advice. In view of the controverted state of the question, it is necessary to evaluate the rationale behind the positions which are held. By considering four disputed interrelated aspects of the overall question and different ways of resolving them the task of moral analysis faced by surrogates who must make decisions about the tube feeding of incompetent wards will become apparent.

FIRST. *Do feeding tubes constitute a medical technology or are they a form of routine comfort care?*

SECOND. *For a nonterminally ill patient who has limited sentience and is severely demented or who is in an irreversible coma or a persistent vegetative state, can the discontinuance of tube feeding be morally justified?*

THIRD. *Might the poor quality of a comatose or severely demented patient's life, given extensive brain damage and loss of the ability to masticate/swallow, be grounds for forgoing/withdrawing artificial nutrition and hydration?*

FOURTH. *If feeding tubes are removed from an incompetent patient, does the patient die from a culpable omission aimed at the patient's death or from an underlying pathology?*

FIRST. *Do feeding tubes constitute a medical technology or are they a form of routine comfort care?*

Some moral authorities have answered this question by saying that feeding tubes are a medical treatment comparable to such life-support devices as respirators and may be withdrawn for the same reasons that ventilators are disconnected. Other moral authorities contend that artificial feeding is properly placed in a different category from strictly medical procedures and should be considered mandatory unless medically contraindicated.

Thomas Shannon and James Walter say that artificial nutrition and hydration is "medical feeding" which differs significantly from the conscious human experience of feeding oneself or being fed:

> To begin with, we have a situation in which the patient is fed and does not eat; the experience is entirely passive. Orderlies or nurses do not deny trays of food to patients nor do they forcibly remove these trays from the hands of patients. Nutrition and hydration are administered to the patient and the body absorbs them; the feeding process is completely involuntary. Second, the symbolism of the meal is utterly absent, even if others are there. There is no meal, only a medical feeding. Though nourishing, it is difficult to consider such a liquid protein diet as food. For food, in addition to having a certain biological reality, is also a human construct and is more than the sum of its nutritional value. It is the color, texture, aroma, taste and company in which it is shared. For the PVS patient, all this is absent. To call this nourishment food is to invest it with more meaning than the reality of the situation can bear.[11]

Richard A. McCormick, S.J., who holds the John A. O'Brien Chair of Moral Theology at the University of Notre Dame, considers the special training needed for caregivers who provide artificial nutrition and hydration to patients an indication that such feeding should be classified as a "strictly medical procedure." Father McCormick writes:

> Most of us would not know how to go about providing nutrition and hydration by nasogastric tube and IV lines. These procedures require skilled medical training. Does that not constitute them

strictly medical procedures? This is an issue because normal
feeding has profound symbolic importance in human relationships
and societal structure. It is one thing to starve the hungry. We
should be appalled at the idea. It is quite another to withhold or
withdraw a medical procedure. That we do routinely and jus-
tifiably.[12]

Kevin D. O'Rourke, O.P., the Director of the Center for Health Care
Ethics of the St. Louis University Medical School, puts artificial feeding in
the same category as Shannon, Walter and McCormick. In Father
O'Rourke's opinion "tube feeding . . . is a life support system rather than a
comfort device."[13] Because it is a "life support system," O'Rourke maintains that noninitiation or discontinuance of tube feeding are reasonable
choices if the honest judgment is made that the time has come to let nature
take its course.[14]

In January, 1987 the New Jersey Catholic Conference[15] submitted a
brief to the New Jersey Supreme Court when that court was hearing arguments regarding whether or not to allow withdrawal of tube feeding from
Nancy Ellen Jobes, a 31 year old nursing home resident who was severely
brain damaged but not terminally ill. The Conference analyzes artificial
feeding as comparable to oral feeding; it contends that tube feeding is not a
medical treatment because medical treatments are aimed at curing
pathologies:

Nutrition and hydration are clearly distinguished from medical
treatment. Medical treatment is aimed at curing a disease. Nutrition and hydration are directed at sustaining life. Medical treatment is therapeutic; nutrition and hydration are not, because they
will not cure any disease. For that fundamental reason we insist
that nutrition and hydration must always be maintained.[16]

An August 3, 1987 directive sent to Catholic hospitals in the
Archdiocese of Newark and signed by Theodore E. McCarrick who serves
as archbishop stated that "nutrition and hydration, when not useless or excessively burdensome, should not ordinarily be withdrawn from non-dying
patients, even if they are unconscious, comatose or in a persistent vegetative state."[17] What seem to be morally decisive in the Conference brief
and the archbishop's statement are the interpretation that artificial feeding

sustains life and that the nondying lives of brain damaged patients should be sustained.

What are the consequences of the fact that the nature of tube feeding is controverted by moral authorities? The most significant consequence is probably the disagreement about whether the distinctions used to evaluate medical treatments, i.e. the ordinary-extraordinary categories and the proportionate-disproportionate criteria, ought to be employed in deciding to continue, discontinue or refuse to initiate such feedings. These distinctions allow patients or their surrogates to make calculations based on burdens and benefits to patients, and in view of such values as the patient's finances, expressed preferences as to care desired if rendered incompetent, or grave burdens which might be experienced by loved ones in connection with a treatment course. If, on the other hand, "nutrition and hydration must always be maintained," as the brief filed on behalf of the bishops of New Jersey maintains, severe limitations would be placed on the exercise of discretion by surrogates. Indeed, the only circumstances under which the forgoing or withdrawing of tube feeding would probably be justified would be a patient's nearness to death and concurrent inability to assimilate feeding or grave pain and suffering experienced in conjunction with tube feeding which cannot be alleviated by available remedies.

SECOND. *For a nonterminally ill patient who has limited sentience and is severely demented or who is in an irreversible coma or a persistent vegetative state, can the discontinuance of tube feeding be morally justified?*

(The noninitiation of artificial feeding is usually not an issue. In emergency circumstances tube feeding is routinely begun. In nonemergency situations time-limited trials are frequently entered into; the possibility of discontinuance is considered if surrogates become convinced that there is virtually no hope for recovery. Less frequently, cases arise in which next of kin witness the steady deterioration of loved ones which culminates in the loss of the ability to swallow. In such cases surrogates may refuse to authorize tube feeding. In the event that the initiation of tube feeding is rejected, the same moral criteria apply as in cases involving its discontinuance.)

Those who respond to the second question in the negative generally propose reasons such as the four which follow as justification for their conclusion:

1. Tube feeding enables incompetent patients to continue living, and life is a great good.

2. Incompetent patients are vulnerable and need the care of others; surrogates and healthcare professionals are morally obligated to render care.

3. Artificially provided food and water preserve the lives of incompetent patients; it would be incorrect to think of this therapy as useless and morally dispensable on the ground that it cannot effect a recovery to consciousness.

4. The provision of food and fluids by feeding tube is not a burden if it does not cause incompetent patients undue pain or suffering; were tube feeding to become a burden, a morally defensible decision could be reached to discontinue it.

In the Winter, 1987 volume of *Issues in Law & Medicine*, seven Roman Catholic moral authorities (William E. May, Robert Barry, O.P., Msgr. Orville Griese, Germain Grisez, Brian Johnstone, C.Ss.R., Bishop James T. McHugh, S.T.D., and Msgr. William Smith) joined by three other prominent persons, Gilbert Meilander, Ph.D. (an ethicist), Thomas J. Marzen, J.D. (an attorney), and Mark Siegler, M.D. (a physician), authored a statement entitled "Feeding and Hydrating the Permanently Unconscious and Other Vulnerable Persons." The writers of this position paper secured the endorsement of ninety-five additional signatories for their position; as it turned out, the original drafters and subsequent signatories represent a number of different religious and ethical traditions. "Feeding and Hydrating the Permanently Unconscious and Other Vulnerable Persons" contains a presentation of the argument against discontinuing the tube feeding of nonterminally ill incompetent patients. Let us consider why the authors hold reasons comparable to the four just enumerated.

William E. May, Professor of Moral Theology at the Catholic University of America, et al., hold that tube feeding allows incompetent patients to continue living and assess this continued living as a great good. They write: "Human bodily life is a great good. . . . It is a good *of* the person, not merely *for* the person. Such life is inherently good, not merely instrumental to other goods."[18] Since artificially provided nutrition and hydration "benefits the nondying patient by serving this fundamental personal good—human life itself—which remains good in itself no matter how burdened it may become due to the patient's poor condition,"[19] tube feeding should not be withdrawn from incompetent patients. By declaring that life is good in itself and rejecting theories that life's goodness depends on a person's being able to enjoy interpersonal relationships, be aware of the environment, being able to carry on meaningful activities, or some other factor, those who collaborated on this article seek to establish unconditional regard for the lives of incompetents and infer that this regard includes an obligation to initiate and continue tube feeding.

In regard to the second reason for saying that discontinuance of tube feeding of nonterminally ill incompetents is not morally justified, May, et al., hold that incompetent patients are vulnerable and that surrogates and healthcare professionals are morally obligated to care for them. They maintain that "caring for others expresses recognition of their personhood, and responds appropriately to it . . . care for a helpless adult—family member, neighbor, or stranger—expresses compassion and humane appreciation of his or her dignity. It also offers the possibility to the caregiver of nurturing such noble qualities as mercy and compassion."[20] And they base the moral obligation of providing feeding on the Golden Rule: "only one who sets aside the Golden Rule will consider excessively burdensome the provision by our society of life-sustaining care to all its members who require it and can benefit from it."[21]

The third reason which is proposed to reject the moral appropriateness of discontinuing tube feeding is that artificially provided food and water preserve the lives of incompetent patients; it would be incorrect to think of this therapy as useless and morally dispensable on the grounds that it cannot effect a recovery to consciousness. The sense in which the term "useless" is correctly understood is explained as follows:

> Plainly, when a person is imminently dying, a time often comes when it is really useless or excessively burdensome to continue hydration and nutrition, whether by tube or otherwise. But the

question that concerns us is not about patients who are judged to be imminently dying, but rather about those who are not.

In our judgment, feeding such patients and providing them with fluids by means of tubes is not useless in the strict sense because it does bring to these patients a great benefit, namely the preservation of their lives and the prevention of their death through malnutrition and dehydration.[22]

It is because artificial feeding preserves life and prevents death that it is considered useful and morally required. The exception to this requirement is stipulated in reason 4.

Reason 4 states that the provision of food and fluids by feeding tube is not a burden if it does not cause incompetent patients undue pain or suffering. In this regard, William E. May, et al., hold that in most situations this is the case:

> We recognize that provision of food and fluids by IVs and nasogastric tubes can have side-effects (e.g., irritation of the nasal passages, sore throats, collapsing veins, etc.) that might become serious enough in particular cases to render their use excessively burdensome. But the experience of many physicians and nurses suggests that these side-effects are often transitory and capable of being ameliorated. Moreover, use of gastic tubes does not ordinarily cause the patient grave discomfort. There may be gas pains, diarrhea, or nose and throat irritation, but ordinarily such discomforts are of passing nature and can be ameliorated. We thus judge that providing food and fluids to the permanently unconscious and other categories of seriously debilitated but nondying persons (e.g., those with strokes or Alzheimer's disease) does not ordinarily impose excessive burdens by reason of pain or damage to bodily self and functioning. Psychological repugnance, restrictions on physical liberty and preferred activities, or harm to the person's mental life are not relevant considerations in the cases with which we are concerned.[23]

As far as the second half of reason 4 is concerned, "were tube feeding to become a burden, a morally defensible decision could be reached to discontinue it," the authors cite two circumstances in which the artificial provision of nutrition and hydration would be useless (or a burden) and could be discontinued:

(a) the person in question is imminently dying, so that any effort to sustain life is futile, or

(b) the person is no longer able to assimilate the nourishment or fluids thus provided.[24]

Our survey of moral reasons 1-4 regarding why a nonterminally ill patient with severe brain impairment should not have tube feeding discontinued contains principles and conclusions which support this position. Whether or not this position is ultimately convincing rests upon the cogency of its rationale along with other relevant considerations. The contention of Roman Catholic moral theologians who argue that discontinuing the tube feeding of nonterminally ill brain damaged incompetents may be morally permissible can likewise be understood by considering the four reasons on which this contention is based. Let us consider the four reasons proposed by these theologians while bearing in mind that at this writing they have not formulated a joint statement similar to the one which appeared in *Issues in Law & Medicine*.

1. Life is a good but the lives of patients who are trapped by the halfway technology of artificial feeding need not be sustained in this way if there is no possibility of recovery.

2. Incompetent, permanently brain damaged patients need care; this care may consist solely in comfort measures; surrogates are not morally obligated to authorize artificial nutrition and hydration.

3. The provision of artificial food and water to nonterminally ill patients who are irreversibly brain damaged may be considered useless or futile because this technology will not enable such patients to recover, and it may be forgone or withdrawn.

4. The provision of food and fluids by feeding tube may be a disproportionate burden if the burden to the patient of enduring the indignities of total dependence and the ongoing trauma experienced by family members

and friends in conjunction with the patient's condition is assessed as greater than the benefits of tube feeding.

Moral theologians who contend that artificial nutrition and hydration which are administered to patients who are irreversibly comatose, in a persistent vegetative state, or minimally sentient and severely brain damaged (perhaps following a major stroke) is a "halfway technology"[25] argue that this technology need not be administered to such patients and that a morally defensible decision can be made to allow them to die. In so contending they are not disputing the fundamental truth that life is a great good but are reasoning that it is not morally required to artificially sustain the severely impaired life of certain brain damaged patients. In a commentary written about the Brophy case, Philip Boyle, O.P., Larry King, M.D., and Kevin O'Rourke, O.P., state that "mere physiologic function does not achieve the purpose of human life."[26] And what is the purpose of human life? Thomas Shannon and James Walter respond:

> Clearly the preservation of life is an important goal of the human community in general and the profession of medicine in particular. Intuitively we know life is valuable and sacred; for were it not, then nothing else would be. Yet, when all is said and done, especially in the Christian framework, life—even human life—is not of ultimate value. Philosophically and politically, we affirm a variety of values that transcend human life: justice, charity, the good of the neighbor, etc. On the basis of these values or for their sake, we can qualify our protection of individual human lives. Theologically, only God is of ultimate value; all else, no matter how good or valuable, must take second place. . .
>
> This perspective reminds us, particularly in the health care context, that while preserving life is a good—and even a great good—biological life is neither the highest value nor a value that holds ultimate claim on us. To make biological life the ultimate value is to forget our real priorities and to create an idol by making a lesser good our ultimate reality.[27]

In reacting against what they consider to be vitalism, persons who endorse the interpretation of theologians such as Shannon and Walter hold that it may be morally permissible for a surrogate to authorize the discontinuance of tube feeding from severely brain damaged patients because these patients are unable to pursue any of the goods of life and because it can be construed as reasonable to free them from the entrapment of medical technology so that they can die in peace.

The second moral reason for allowing discontinuance of tube feeding from certain classes of incompetent patients is based upon an understanding of the type of care which is owed to brain damaged incompetents. In this connection, no moral theologian denies that care is owed to vulnerable persons, but many do not assume that care requires artificial feeding for patients who are irreversibly brain damaged. John J. Paris, S.J., a Professor of medical ethics at the College of the Holy Cross, the University of Massachusetts and Tufts Medical School, argues that the principle that no one is obliged to use useless remedies applies to tube feeding.[28] Accordingly, Father Paris contends that surrogates are morally required to employ technologies which offer substantial hope of benefit to a ward,[29] but forms of treatment which do not offer such hope are optional.

Kevin O'Rourke says that, if a decision is made by a surrogate not to initiate or to discontinue tube feeding for a permanently brain damaged patient, pain will probably not be experienced by the patient but, "if it is, it may be alleviated through analgesics."[30] The care which should be provided for patients for whom tube feeding is not initiated or is discontinued is called "comfort care." This care consists in providing medication to control pain as well as positioning the patient and keeping the body clean and lips and mouth moist. Providing such care, as well as being present at the bedside, enable the well to extend mercy and compassion to the vulnerable.

In regard to reason 3, some moral theologians argue that the provision of artificial nutrition via feeding tubes to nonterminally ill patients who are permanently brain damaged is useless (futile) because this technology will not enable such patients to recover. Those who argue in this way assume that artificial feeding is a medical technology and that severely impaired biological life is not an absolute value to be sustained at all costs. They go on to reason that only medical means which offer a reasonable hope of benefit, i.e. restoration to health (including brain function), are morally mandatory. They contend that both their assumptions and conclusions are consistent with Catholic medical-ethical tradition.

Richard A. McCormick, S.J., and John J. Paris, S.J., argue this position in "The Catholic Tradition on the Use of Nutrition and Fluids" which appeared in *America* on May 2, 1987. They relate that the concept of ordinary and extraordinary means has been an integral part of Catholic morality since the sixteenth century,[31] and contend that the Church's consistent teaching since then has been that there is no obligation to use a medical treatment which does not offer substantial benefit to the patient. In other words, there is never an obligation to use an extraordinary means. McCormick and Paris say that the purpose of medicine is to check or cure disease and that available treatments should be evaluated in the light of these possibilities.[32] From their point of view, therapies which are capable only of prolonging a patient's life without ameliorating underlying pathologies, such as artificially provided nutrition and hydration, need not be used.

A statement by the widely respected Catholic moralist, Gerald Kelly, S.J., who wrote for *Theological Studies* in the 1940s and 50s, was cited by McCormick and Paris as supportive of their reasoning and conclusion: "I see no reason why even the most delicate professional standard should call for their use (oxygen and intravenous feeding to extend the life of a patient in a terminal coma). In fact, it seems to me that, apart from very special circumstances, the artificial means not only need not but should not be used, once the coma is reasonably diagnosed as terminal. Their use creates expense and nervous strain without conferring any real benefit."[33] In addition, McCormick and Paris challenged the contention put forth by some moral commentators that artificially sustained existence constitutes a "benefit" for a patient: "to count mere vegetative existence as a patient benefit is to let slip one's grasp on the heart of the Catholic tradition on this matter."[34]

Reason 4 for allowing the discontinuance of artificial nutrition and hydration from nonterminally ill patients who are irreversibly brain damaged states that if the burdens to the patient of enduring the indignities of his/her condition along with the trauma experienced by loved ones can be assessed as greater than the benefits experienced from tube feeding, discontinuance of tube feeding is a morally appropriate option. One aspect of this argument is that the biological life which continues because tube feeding sustains an individual need not be construed as a "benefit" to the patient. In this regard Thomas Shannon and James Walter write:

> . . . because of the overall condition of the patient, when a proposed intervention cannot offer the patient any reasonable hope of pursuing life's purposes at all or can only offer the patient a condition where the pursuit of life's purposes will be filled with profound frustration or with utter neglect of these purposes because of the energy needed merely to sustain physical life, then any medical intervention (1) can only offer burden to the life treated, (2) is contrary to the best interests of the patient, (3) can cause iatrogenic harm or the risk of such harm, and (4) has reached its limit based on medicine's own principal reason for existence, and thus treatment should not be given except to palliate or to comfort.[35]

Accordingly, Shannon, Walter and moral authorities who reason as they do consider the irreversibly brain damaged patient who is kept alive by artificial sustenance to be an individual who is burdened or entrapped by the treatment, kept from crossing the threshold into the next life and not aided by medical technology to fulfill any of the purposes of human existence.

A second aspect of reason 4 is the fact that the trauma experienced by family members and friends is properly included within the overall disproportion associated with the tube feeding of an irreversibly brain damaged incompetent. Andrew C. Varga, S.J., Professor of medical ethics at Fordham University, testified to this effect before the Supreme Court of the State of New York, Appellate Division, in the case of Daniel Delio, a patient in a chronic vegetative state with no hope for improvement. The court record states:

> Father Varga testified that the discontinuance of nutrition and hydration presently furnished to Daniel by artificial means would be ethical and in accordance with Vatican Doctrine since Daniel's condition is irreversible and *maintaining him in his present condition places an enormous burden on his family both economically and emotionally.*[36]

THIRD: *Might the poor quality of a comatose or severely demented patient's life—given extensive brain damage and loss of the ability to masticate/swallow—be grounds for forgoing/withdrawing artificial nutrition and hydration?*

There is fundamental agreement among Roman Catholic moral theologians that each and every human life is sacred and that personal and human dignity are not diminished in any way by physical or mental disability. There is also concurrence that it would be morally wrong to base decisions to forgo or withdraw nutrition and hydration on a consideration such as the social worth of a disabled person who is unable to function in society. Indeed, criteria such as social worth or social productivity are totally rejected as bases upon which decisions ought to be made.

In spite of agreement on these matters, however, there is disagreement about whether or not the quality of a brain damaged patient's life should come into consideration when decisions are made about forgoing and withdrawing tube feeding. The late John R. Connery, S.J., who was Professor of theology at Loyola University of Chicago, thought that it should not. In 1986, Father Connery wrote that "The argument is that life in itself can be so burdensome or so empty that it ceases to be of value, or at least that its value is not sufficient to impose an obligation on the victim to preserve it."[37] Connery expressed an uneasiness about the way the deliberations of U.S. courts in such cases as the Barber-Nejdl case seemed to be moving, and he took particular exception to the way in which Richard A. McCormick, S.J., and John J. Paris, S.J., included the quality of life of irreversibly brain damaged patients as a criterion in moral evaluation. Father Connery maintained that an implicit or explicit willingness to judge some lives to be "so burdensome or so empty" that there is no moral requirement to treat them[38] would essentially be at odds with Catholic medical ethical tradition and should be strongly resisted. He also warned that accepting the quality of life of an irreversibly brain damaged patient as a relevant factor in medical moral decision making could put ethicists on a slippery slope in which the movement from allowing the discontinuance of tube feeding of comatose patients to that of denying the same therapy to patients with Alzheimer's disease, thence to others with mental or physical handicaps, could quickly come.[39]

Most moral theologians who consider it morally appropriate to forgo or withdraw artificial nutrition and hydration from severely and irreversibly brain damaged incompetents reason that it is not the quality of the patient's life per se, but, rather, the potential of the medical treatment to effect recovery to a state of health (the quality of the patient's life with/as a result of the treatment) which is the morally relevant consideration. In this connection, Richard J. Devine, C.M., Associate Professor of theology at Saint John's University (New York), writes:

> ... quality of life considerations need to be a factor in all responsible health care decisions. It is not simply the burdensome treatment (quality of treatment) that may be ethically refused; the burdensome life (quality of life) that continues after the treatment may also justify the decision to forgo a medical procedure.[40]

Father Devine responds to the "slippery slope" argument by contending that the fact that some irresponsibly urge discontinuing care for whole classes of highly vulnerable individuals does not justify a solution that denies the right to refuse artificial nutrition and hydration when there is no proportion between the benefits and the burdens.[41] In Devine's view, when the burdens of artificial feeding outweigh the benefits it brings to a patient, it is morally appropriate to discontinue tube feeding.[42]

Richard A. McCormick argues in the same vein as Father Devine and contends that "the burden-benefit calculus may include, indeed often unavoidably includes, a quality of life ingredient"[43] which is separate and distinct from an analysis of a mode of treatment and its ability to sustain the life of a patient. This "quality of life" ingredient "would seem to consist in the nature of the life experienced by the patient whose brain injury totally precludes the possibility of any degree of mental-creative function"[44] and who can anticipate absolutely no improvement in condition. Because no medical treatment can improve the quality of such a severely diminished life, many moral theologians maintain that there is no moral obligation for either the patient or surrogate to continue medical treatment which merely sustains life without being able to offer the hope of recovery of health.

FOURTH. *If feeding tubes are removed from an incompetent patient, does the patient die from a culpable omission aimed at the patient's death, or from an underlying pathology?*

The moral analysis of human actions consists in a careful evaluation of what is done (the object of the act), why it is done (the intention) and the morally relevant circumstances. Let us consider two possible situations in which the tube feeding of a patient in a persistent vegetative state is discontinued.

Situation 1:

What is done: A feeding tube is removed from a patient in a persistent vegetative state; nursing care is provided for the patient until death comes.

Why it is done: To allow the patient to die of existing pathologies which include the inability to eat and the absence of all brain function other than that of the brain stem.

Morally relevant circumstances: The patient's condition is irreversible and, without the artificial life-support of tube feeding, the patient would actually be dying. The surrogate feels certain that the decision to discontinue tube feeding is consistent with the patient's preferences and/or best interests.

Situation 2:

What is done: A feeding tube is removed from a patient in a persistent vegetative state; nursing care is provided for the patient until death comes.

Why it is done: In order to have the patient die of malnutrition and dehydration.

Morally relevant circumstances: The patient's condition is irreversible and, without the artificial life-support of tube feeding, the patient would actually be dying. The surrogate considers the poor condition of the patient's life an indication of the fact that the biological life which remains is worthless, and need not be preserved.

The second situation differs from the first in two significant regards. One is the conviction of the surrogate decision maker that the poor quality of a ward's life renders that life worthless. As we saw in connection with the discussion of quality of life above, it is morally wrong to form such a conviction because the biological and personal value of the lives of vulnerable persons should always be respected. Through thinking of the life of a person in a persistent vegetative state as worthless, a surrogate would be denying the dignity and sacredness of a vulnerable person; such an attitude is morally inappropriate.

The other way in which the second situation differs from the first is in regard to intentionality. In the second scenario the surrogate requests discontinuance of tube feeding so that the patient will die of malnutrition and dehydration. One could say that the surrogate is aiming at death and that caretakers are carrying out this aim. If this in fact is the intention for what is done, the action would be morally wrong because it is ethically wrong to aim at or directly intend an evil, and death is a physical evil. Gilbert Meilander, Ph.D., an Associate Professor at Oberlin College, makes precisely this point; Dr. Meilander's analysis was endorsed by the New Jersey Catholic Conference in its brief on the Jobes case:

> Nor can we, when withdrawing food from the permanently unconscious person, properly claim that our intention is to cease useless treatment for a dying patient. These patients are not dying, and we cease no treatment aimed at disease; rather, we withdraw the nourishment that sustains all human beings, whether healthy or ill, and we do so when the only result of our action can be death. At what, other than death, could we be aiming?[45]

Moral theologians who assess situation 1 as an ethically reasonable course to follow would concur with Meilander that it is wrong to aim at death. They would differ with him, however, in maintaining that it is not morally wrong to intend to allow a patient to die of underlying pathologies and to evaluate tube feeding as an optional life-support system which offers no benefit to the brain damaged patient, provided that the patient's previously expressed preferences or best interests be given due account. Richard Devine states the position well:

... the patient in kidney failure is not dying so long as dialysis is continued, but a decision to terminate treatment may be justified—even though death will surely follow—if the burdens to a particular individual become disproportionate to the benefits. Death is not what is willed, even though it follows from the withdrawal decision, and with certitude. What is intended is to cease using a procedure that offers less benefit than burden and to accept the foreseen physical consequences, without intending them. Nowhere does either Dr. Meilander or the brief explain why the patient in a persistent vegetative state, who is not dying so long as artificial nutrition and hydration are provided, is different from the patient needing artificial support for respiration or renal function. Why allow this exception to the principles that moralists have broadly accepted? Why deny the burden/benefit calculus to the permanently unconscious person with respect only to sustenance?[46]

If a comatose patient dies as a result of a decision to terminate tube feeding because sustenance thus provided is more of a burden than a benefit to the patient, it is possible that a question might arise as to whether the patient's death is the result of an act of omission or commission, and, if the conclusion is that the patient died as a result of an omission, whether or not the omission was morally justified. An act of commission consists in doing something intentionally to bring about a change or doing something to prevent a change from taking place. An omission consists in leaving something unchanged or allowing something to happen. In its policy against euthanasia, Catholic moral tradition is unequivocal in condemning the taking of innocent human life or failure to act to bring restoration of health to sick persons when it is possible for individuals or society as a whole to do so.

In regard to omissions, a person can be guilty of an omission only if the person has the ability to perform a particular action, if the person has an opportunity to perform it, and if there is a reasonable expectation that the person is morally required to perform it. In respect to the third criterion, the writers of "Feeding and Hydrating the Permanently Unconscious and other Vulnerable Persons" affirm that there is a reasonable expectation that the permanently unconscious will be tube fed, and assess omission of such feeding in a very negative manner:

> Certain people claim to oppose euthanasia and do not advocate killing by acts of commission, but nevertheless support the view that treatment may rightly be withheld or withdrawn from noncompetent nonterminal persons simply because their lives are thought by others to be valueless or excessively burdensome. . . . It is cause for very great alarm that some influential physicians, ethicists, and courts have adopted this rationale for withholding or withdrawing food and fluids—and other means of preserving life—from some persons. For in adopting this rationale, they approve and legally sanction euthanasia by omission—deliberate killing—in these cases.[47]

As we have seen, the determination to discontinue artificial feeding need not rest on the assumption that the lives of persons so sustained are valueless. It is also evident that forgoing or withdrawing medical feeding so as to allow a patient to die of underlying pathologies need not be assessed as "euthanasia by omission—deliberate killing" which of course would be morally reprehensible. Thomas Shannon and James Walter offer a rejoinder to William E. May, et al:

> A moral analysis of euthanasia necessarily involves an assessment of the intention. Though they may be motivated by humane reasons, morally all acts of euthanasia intend the death of the patient either by commission or by omission, and thus by definition these acts constitute the unjustified killing of a patient. However, we argue that in withdrawing nutrition and hydration the intent is either to end a procedure that no longer benefits the patient or to prevent the person from being entrapped in technology. The patient's death, while foreseen, results from the justified discontinuance of a technology that itself can neither correct the underlying fatal pathology, i.e. the permanent inability to ingest food and fluids orally, nor offer the patient any reasonable hope for what we have defined as quality of life. In our judgment, then, it is inappropriate to characterize the withdrawal of

medical nutrition and hydration from PVS patients as euthanasia.[48]

It is apparent that there is significant disagreement within the ranks of Catholic moral authorities on the nature of tube feeding, the moral evaluation of discontinuing tube feeding from patients who are permanently brain damaged, how "quality of life" figures in decisions to discontinue treatment, and how to assess the intention and the object of the action when artificial feeding is forgone or discontinued. Given this disagreement, and in view of the very complicated aspects of moral decisions faced by surrogates, it is necessary to determine how they should go about making decisions on behalf of dependent wards.

Because of the lack of agreement among moral authorities in the Catholic Church in the United States at the present time, surrogates are sometimes burdened with the task of carefully considering the different conclusions which are put forward by these authorities as well as the rationale supporting their conclusions. After weighing the arguments on both sides of the issue, surrogates bear the awesome responsibility of reaching decisions to initiate, forgo, continue or discontinue tube feeding. Their decisions will reflect the way in which they interpret what tube feeding does and what happens when tube feeding is not initiated or is discontinued. How they understand their obligation to honor the advance directives of their wards, or to act in their best interests, are also critically important aspects of the decision making process.

Given the impasse between moral authorities, one thing is certain. At the present time whichever course surrogates choose to follow can be ethically defended provided it is chosen in good faith following thorough reflection. In my opinion the current lack of agreement among moral authorities will probably continue for the forseeable future because this disagreement touches such fundamental matters as the nature of tube feeding and the applicability of traditional distinctions in cases involving nonterminally ill and irreversibly brain damaged patients. Reaching agreement on this controverted question, however, may be facilitated by considering the advice given by Joseph Cardinal Bernardin along with the spiritual and psychological anguish endured by people of good will who are thrust by fate into situations in which they must make decisions for loved ones:

. . . the controverted question of the artificial provision of nutrition and hydration for several categories of patients needs to be resolved. We cannot accept a policy that would open the door to euthanasia by creating categories of patients whose lives can be considered of no value merely because they are not conscious. We also may not develop a policy to keep alive those who should be allowed a natural death, that is, those who are terminally ill, or to preclude a decision—informed by our ethical principles and on a case by case basis—that the artificial provision of nutrition and hydration has become useless or unduly burdensome.

I know that this is a very complex issue. I am convinced that, from a moral point of view, the essential bond between food, water, and life argues convincingly for the presumption that nutrition and hydration should always be provided. But I am also convinced that we are not *morally* obliged to do everything that is *technically* possible. In other words, there are cases where we would not be obliged artifically to provide nutrition and hydration. The challenge is to develop a nuanced public policy to protect against an attitude that could erode respect for the inviolable dignity of human life. If we do not resolve this critical issue in a way which resonates with the common sense of people of good will, then we may contribute to the sense of desperation that will lead people to consider euthanasia as an alternative solution to the problem.[49]

Conclusion

Technology has made it possible to maintain the biological life of patients who suffer permanent brain damage, leaving them unaware of their surroundings and unable to interact with others. In addition, some severely demented patients are restrained in order to be tube fed; bed sores may add to the discomfort they experience, and they run the risk of developing pneumonia and other complications. Physicians, hospital and nursing home administrators and next of kin of incompetent patients are sometimes faced with decisions about initiation or noninitiation, continuing or discontinuing tube feeding. They want to know in what the morally correct approach consists, so that they can do the right thing in behalf of persons who are in a very vulnerable condition. As we have seen in this chapter, moral decisions involving artificial nutrition and hydration are among the most complex choices that people have to make. While the Roman Catholic medical moral tradition offers valuable insight and guidance to decision makers, given the disagreement among Catholic moral authorities on several specific aspects of the tube feeding of incompetents, each individual who is confronted with this issue must bear the burden of taking the responsibility for resolving it by himself or herself.

Endnotes

1. Joseph Cardinal Bernardin, "The Consistent Ethic of Life and Health Care Systems," May 8, 1985, in Joseph Cardinal Bernardin, *Consistent Ethic of Life* (Kansas City, MO: Sheed & Ward, 1988) p. 51.

2. Gerald Kelly, *Medico Moral Problems* (St. Louis, MO: Catholic Health Association, 1958), p. 129.

3. Pope Pius XII, AAS 49 (1957).

4. Sacred Congregation for the Doctrine of the Faith, *Declaration on Euthanasia* (Boston: Daughters of St. Paul, 1980), p. 11.

5. Ibid.

6. Ibid.

7. Ibid., p. 12.

8. Given the technological sophistication of modern medical science, it is possible to focus just about exclusively on ailments and treatment alternatives, forgetting one's needs, values and desires. A person at the end of a protracted battle with cancer, for example, should feel free to reject an experimental treatment and additional hospitalization so as to return home even if such a choice is likely to result in an earlier death. The total human good of the dying person who wants the closeness of family and friends and the comfort of familiar surroundings is frequently of greater value than managing and/or treating an end-stage disease.

9. Thomas A. Shannon and James J. Walter, "The PVS Patient and the Forgoing/Withdrawing of Medical Nutrition and Hydration," *Theological Studies,* December, 1988, 49:4, p. 625.

10. Ibid.

11. Ibid., pp. 642, 643.

12. Richard A. McCormick, S.J., "Caring or Starving? The Case of Claire Conroy," *America*, April 6, 1985, 152:13, p. 272.

13. Kevin D. O'Rourke, O.P., "Tube Feeding—Routine Nursing Care?" *Parameters 83,* Summer, 1985, 8:2, p. 18.

14. Ibid.

15. The New Jersey Catholic Conference is composed of the Roman Catholic bishops of the Archdiocese of Newark, the Dioceses of Camden, Metuchen, Paterson, Trenton and the Byzantine Catholic Diocese of Passaic. The Conference provides a means by which bishops may speak on matters of public policy. The brief which the Conference submitted to the court was written by William F. Bolan, Esq.

16. New Jersey State Catholic Conference Brief, "Providing Food and Fluids to Severely Brain Damaged Patients," *Origins,* January 22, 1987, 16:32, p. 583.

17. Most Rev. Theodore E. McCarrick, Archbishop of Newark, (letter to Catholic hospitals), August 3, 1987, p. 2. Note use of the words "should not ordinarily be withdrawn," which suggest that there may be extraordinary cases in which feeding tubes may be withdrawn. In spite of several telephone calls to the Communications Office of the Archdiocese of Newark and one phone conversation with Bishop James T. McHugh (fomerly of the Archdiocese of Newark), I was unable to obtain clarification as to what such extraordinary cases might be and whether or not these might include cases in which tube feeding is rejected because futile in restoring health to a severely debilitated and demented stroke patient or a patient in a persistent vegetative state.

18. William E. May, Robert Barry, O.P., Msgr. Orville Griese, Germain Grisez, Brian Johnstone, C.Ss.R., Thomas J. Marzen, J.D., Bishop James T. McHugh, STD., Gilbert Meilaender, Ph.D., Mark Siegler, M.D., Msgr. William Smith, "Feeding and Hydrating the Permanently Unconscious and Other Vulnerable Persons," *Issues in Law & Medicine,* Winter, 1987, 3:3, p. 204.

19. Ibid., p. 210.

20. Ibid., pp. 210, 211.

21. Ibid., p. 211.

22. Ibid., p. 209

23. Ibid., pp. 209, 210.

24. Ibid., p. 209.

25. John J. Paris, SJ, "When Burdens of Feeding Outweigh Benefits," *Hastings Center Report,* February, 1986, 16:1, p. 31.

26. Philip Boyle, OP, Larry King, MD, and Kevin O'Rourke, OP, "The Brophy Case: The Use of Artificial Hydration and Nutrition," *Linacre Quarterly,* May, 1987, 22:18, p. 71.

27. Op. cit., Shannon, Walter, pp. 633, 634.

28. Op. cit., Paris, p. 32.

29. Ibid.

30. Op. cit., O'Rourke, p. 18.

31. John J. Paris, SJ, and Richard A. McCormick, SJ, "The Catholic Tradition on the Use of Nutrition and Fluids," *America*, May 2, 1987, 156:17, p. 358.

32. Ibid., p. 361.

33. Ibid., p. 359.

34. Ibid., p. 361.

35. Op. cit., Shannon, Walter, p. 645.

36. In the Matter of Julianne Delio, The Supreme Court of the State of New York, Appellate Division: Second Department, 1391 PZ/eb, June 1, 1987, p. 11, italics added.

37. John R. Connery, SJ, "The Quality of Life," *Linacre Quarterly*, February, 1986, 53:1, p. 30.

38. Ibid.

39. Ibid., p. 32.

40. Richard J. Devine, CM, "The Amicus Curiae Brief: Public Policy Versus Personal Freedom," *America*, April 8, 1989, 160:13, p. 326.

41. Ibid., p. 334.

42. Ibid., p. 326.

43. Op. cit., McCormick, p. 273.

44. Op cit., O'Rourke, p. 17.

45. Gilbert Meilander, "Caring for the Permanently Unconscious Patient," in Joanne Lynn, *By No Extraordinary Means* (Bloomington, IN: Indiana University Press, 1986), p. 197; cf., Brief, p. 583.

46. Op. cit., Devine, p. 325.

47. Op. cit., May, pp. 206, 207.

48. Op. cit., Shannon, Walter, p. 641.

49. Joseph Cardinal Bernardin, Address: "Euthanasia: Ethical and Legal Challenge," University of Chicago Hospital, May 26, 1988.

4

Making Decisions
Regarding Artificial
Nutrition and Hydration:
A Very Difficult Process

Introduction

It is difficult to make decisions about artificial nutrition and hydration. It is less difficult, however, to make decisions for oneself than to do so for someone else. Competent patients have opportunities to ask questions, negotiate with physicians and commit themselves to one or another course; based upon their experience of being tube fed and the outcomes it brings, they are also free to continue or discontinue its use. They have the satisfaction of knowing that there are legal safeguards which allow them to exercise self-determination and they know that they act in an ethical manner if they sincerely judge the choice they make to be reasonable. In a sense, competent patients answer to themselves; unless there is a question as to their ability to exercise competence, the various institutions of society respect their decisions and refrain from intruding upon their autonomy. In addition, competent patients who authorize enteral or parenteral nutrition do so knowing that they cannot absorb sufficient nourishment by mouth and that their continued ability to exercise competence as well as their continued existence depend upon feeding administered through tubes.

When surrogates make decisions for incompetents, the surrogates may feel insecure because of the role in which they find themselves. As we saw in the preceding chapters, some religious and ethical leaders and a few judges seem to be moving in a vitalist direction. Even if they are acting in accord with a patient's advance directive or on behalf of a patient's best interests, surrogates who decide that forgoing or withdrawing nutrition is the proper course may feel some anxiety and insecurity based on such decisions as the one reached by the New York State Court of Appeals in the O'Connor case and the position taken by the authors and signatories of "Feeding and Hydrating the Permanently Unconscious and Other Vulnerable Persons." They may also feel depressed and burdened because the nonfeeding of a loved one will unfailingly result in death.

On the other hand, those who authorize tube feeding may feel troubled too. Knowing how diminished life is when a patient cannot communicate, move about or care for himself or herself will likely cause feelings of bewilderment and frustration as well as uneasiness about exercising jurisdiction in what was until relatively recently the exclusive domain of fate. As competent persons prevent their incompetent wards from dying, these surrogate decision makers may come to resent the technology which cheats nature and which makes a vastly diminished mode of existence possible.

Whether the decision reached on behalf of an incompetent is for or against artificial feeding, the reality which a loved one faces is bleak. This is because incompetent tube fed patients (both the severely demented and those in a persistent vegetative state) can no longer communicate and because in virtually all cases they will not be able to engage in enjoyable activities in the future. Those who grieve go through a difficult time; next of kin of patients in a persistent vegetative state or those with severe and irreversible mental disabilities begin the process of grieving prior to death. What insights will bring them resignation and peace? How are they to cope with the extraordinarily stressful situations in which they find themselves? The purpose of this chapter is to suggest responses to questions such as these.

Insight About the Meanings of Life and Death

The Myth of Sisyphus, written by Albert Camus (1913-1960), a very influential French writer and thinker, describes the ordeal which occupied Sisyphus during his lifetime. Sisyphus, the wisest of mortals, had stolen the secrets of the gods. As punishment, the gods condemned Sisyphus to spend his days rolling a large rock to the top of a mountain, and then watching it fall back of its own weight. This scenario was repeated time after time for as long as Sisyphus lived.

Sisyphus was Camus' metaphor for each person. Camus believed that each individual struggles, achieves only limited success, and suffers ultimate failure when claimed by death. Catholic Christians are challenged by such thought-provoking accounts as *The Myth of Sisyphus* to confront the sadness, failure and frustration inherent in life and death and to determine why, in spite of limitation and suffering, life and death hold meaning and promise.

The human condition is the less than perfect state of being in which people have to earn their bread by the sweat of their brow without the assurance that they will enjoy a long, happy and prosperous retirement when their days of toil are over. As individuals grow to maturity they find themselves searching for elusive answers to the so-called ultimate questions. When will I know peace? What is life's meaning? Why do good people suffer? Why are tornadoes and diseases a part of nature? How can God be close to me when I feel so much anguish and am tempted to give up hope? Christians believe that the restlessness and confusion which everyone experiences to one degree or another will come to an end when this earthly life ends and eternal life begins. In the words of the great fourth century theologian Saint Augustine, "Our hearts are restless, O! Lord, and they will not rest until they rest in thee." In marked contrast to the nihilistic philosophy of Camus, Christians hope that the promise contained in the book of Revelation will come true:

> Never again shall they know
>   hunger or thirst,
> nor shall the sun or its heat
>   beat down on them,
> for the lamb on the throne
>   will shepherd them.
> He will lead them to
> springs of lifegiving water
>   and God will wipe away
> every tear from their eyes.
>   (Rev. 7:16-17)

In spite of their beliefs it is difficult for Christians to find meaning for death within the context of contemporary culture which prizes youth, strength, vitality and beauty, and which tries in a multitude of ways to deny the reality of death. We may be tempted to think that if we could negotiate the terms on which we would accept death it would be more palatable. The death which comes speedily to pleasantly senile octogenarians who have played with great grandchildren, enjoyed good health and prosperity throughout their lives, and come to real intimacy with God during their golden years does not seem like a very fearsome thing. But deaths out of season, deaths for which people are unprepared, and deaths which follow months or years of pain and suffering or comatose existence seem especially distasteful. The modern technology which has brought us space flights, computers, pacemakers—and artificial nutrition and hydration—impacts with increasing frequency on the way in which we die. The accomplishments of our technological civilization have a dual result: life-saving and life-prolonging techniques make it easier for us to deny that death has power over us while simultaneously making it much more difficult for us to die.

The Christian faith teaches that life holds promise of limited satisfaction and that death comes on its own terms. The most mature among us can accept the fact that we will die, and understand the connection between death and sin. Why are mortals ultimately powerless before death, and why does the separation caused by death engender so much pain? In another place I suggest the following as a response to this profound question:

> The Christian faith teaches that death as we know it is a consequence of sin. Sin is part and parcel of the human condition. Each and every human person commits sins, and, even before the commission of concrete, personal sins, men and women are aware of a brokenness or division within themselves. The weakened condition which is actualized in sinful deeds is called original sin. The theological notion of original sin is very complex but one of the simplest ways of explaining it is to say that it is the shared human tendency to pride, disobedience, and rebelliousness toward God. The pain and anguish which are experienced in connection with death are a consequence of the original sin which affects all humans. If men and women did not consider themselves wiser

than God, if they did not seek their own satisfaction at the expense of their neighbors, and if they were not so lazy and self-centered, theologians speculate that death would not be a traumatic experience.[1]

Jesus' purchase of redemption for humankind through his death on the cross, and his promise that believers will share in the fruits of his resurrection from the dead complete the context within which believers understand death. In spite of doubts, believers hold onto the conviction that death is a threshhold and that, following death, they will attain the kind of happiness alluded to by Saint Paul:

> Eye has not seen, ear has not heard, nor has it so much as dawned
> on humankind what God has prepared for those who love him.
>
> (1 Cor. 2:9)

Camus used Sisyphus to teach the lesson that life is ultimately absurd. The shallow contemporary philosophy of "me first" suggests that life is a period of time to be used for accumulating material things and enjoying pleasures, and contradicts the Great Commandment proposed by Jesus which requires that his followers love God and their neighbors as well as themselves (Matt 22:37-39). Christians differ from both the nihilists and the self-indulgent because they understand that life has a purpose and that death, in spite of its sting, is the doorway to eternal fulfillment. The Christian view of life and death provides a valuable perspective within which to consider decisions about artificial nutrition and hydration.

How Christian Beliefs Influence Decisions about Artificial Nutrition and Hydration

People are profoundly influenced by their religious beliefs. In regard to the meaning of life and death Christian beliefs lead to attitudes and convictions which affect the way people live and die. While it is not possible to establish that certain beliefs always and inevitably result in particular choices, it is possible to indicate the general thrust of the insight which characterizes Christian conviction and the way this insight affects decisions about the care of the dying.

Christian teaching values life as a gift from God and understands that God's intention is that people live together in community. Able-bodied persons are expected to assist the sick and all those in need. Even though the suffering of the sick as well as their loved ones takes on meaning and purpose when it is united to the suffering Christ offered in obedience to God, care of the suffering and dying requires that every available palliative measure be offered to them. While technology has contributed to progress, it cannot deliver humankind from the frailty and limitations of the human condition. Physical and psychological suffering are part of the human condition and, regardless of efforts to prevent it or hold it at bay, death will eventually come to each and every person. Just as there is a time to be born, there is a time to die. Accepting this truth and allowing death to come (but never causing death by overt acts) makes good sense, especially in view of the fact that Christians believe that a new life replete with fulfillment and peace awaits them.

When believing Christians make decisions about nutrition and hydration, they are influenced by their beliefs and guided by them. In regard to decisions competent persons make for themselves, these beliefs allow for the exercise of a significant amount of discretion provided that there is a reverent attitude toward life and a trust in God's promise of immortality. Unfortunately, however, these beliefs do not eliminate the ambiguity attendant to decision making on behalf of an incompetent ward. Since Christians are responsible to love and care for those in need, especially those to whom they are joined by ties of blood or friendship, and to extend to them available palliative measures, Christian beliefs require the determination of what appropriate care consists in. It is also necessary to evaluate how the dying process is experienced by patients who are tube fed for as long as possible and by those for whom artificial feeding is discontinuted. Persons who must decide whether or not to authorize artificial feeding will need to rely upon data provided by medical science as well as anecdotal evidence related by physicians and other healthcare professionals. In regard to persons who are in a persistent vegetative state, the consensus is that they feel nothing, and hence would not suffer were tube feeding to be discontinued. In regard to patients for whom death is expected within a matter of hours or, at most, a few days, dehydration is thought to have a tranquilizing effect.[2] According to the opinion of many moral theologians, in these two types of cases, guardians who decide to forgo or withdraw artificial feeding would not be violating fundamental Christian ethical and religious values.

A much more perplexing case is presented by severely demented, sentient patients who are not terminally ill. Does nonfeeding of such persons cause them to die of hunger and thirst? And are "hunger and thirst" as experienced by such patients comparable to the agony suffered by people stranded on a desert or by famine victims? If so, of course it would be wrong to deny artificial sustenance to these severely demented patients. But if these incompetent patients would experience nonfeeding in the same way as it is experienced by people who are actually in the process of dying, and if it seems wrong to prevent them from realizing the peace which death holds for them, then Christian religious convictions do not preclude deciding to allow them to die. What may stand in the way of reaching such a conclusion is the fact that there remains a degree of ambiguity about the way dying is experienced by severely demented patients. (Dresser and Boisaubin, Schmitz and O'Brien, who are cited in Chapter One, offer clincal observations which support the conclusion that malnutrition and dehydration can actually enhance the experience of dying. However, when pressed to give a definitive answer as to what a severely demented patient would experience if feeding were discontinued, Dr. Wasserman, testifying in the O'Connor case, replied that he could not say with certitude, thus leaving a doubt.) If the decision of a surrogate is to allow an incompetent severely demented patient to forgo tube feeding, justification for this decision will probably be located in the rational and intuitive judgment that the benefits to the patient of continued living are less than the burdens of the severely limited life the patient is enduring. This judgment will likely go hand-in-hand with a willingness to allow the pathologies which afflict the patient (such as an inability to swallow) to take their course.

Assisting Persons Who Must Decide about Artificial Nutrition and Hydration

The Roman Catholic moral tradition has always respected the personal right to act in accordance with the light of a well formed conscience. At one and the same time this tradition has affirmed the freedom of individuals to make their own decisions and has charged them with bearing responsibility for the choices they make. In respect to decisions about artificial sustenance for oneself or another, individuals reluctantly choose between heart-rending alternatives. Because of the dynamics in the clinical scenarios surrounding use and nonuse of feeding tubes, neither competent patients nor surrogates are able to sidestep their responsibilities when decisions seem too momentous, or to turn decision making over to others when levels of anxiety are very high. As a result, it is apparent that people who make decisions about tube feeding find themselves in very stressful situations and could benefit from several kinds of supportive assistance.

Physicians play a major supportive role in assisting patients and surrogates. John Edward Ruark, M.D., and Thomas Alfred Raffin, M.D., offer an appraisal of the physician's task:

> Physicians should act as consultants engaged to evaluate their patient's problems, present reasonable options for treatment in understandable language, and facilitate decision making. Except in emergencies, doctors should feel permitted to proceed with treatments only after those with true authority have clearly decided.[3]

Physicians should not assume that the information they need to communicate can be assimilated in one sitting. It is often hard to accept medical diagnoses which are accompanied by poor prognoses and more than one meeting may be required for patients and/or next of kin to grasp objective medical data and ask questions. Changes in clinical status require reassessments of treatment plans; sometimes tube feeding appears indicated at one point in an illness but becomes contraindicated as the illness proceeds or the use of a feeding tube itself becomes problematic. Physicians serve their patients to the extent that they are willing to give the time it takes to relate the expert knowledge they possess, to clarify misconceptions, and to answer questions. They do not act in a professional manner if they act on the basis of unfounded assumptions or if they impose their own ideas or values. In all cases, tact is called for. As Drs. Ruark and Raffin remark:

> The balance between the probable extension of life and the reduction in quality of life resulting from any treatment must be explicitly described and discussed with each patient. Absolute candor about the level of discomfort associated with any anticipated

treatment is essential, but emotional coldness or brutal abruptness should be avoided.[4]

When decisions about tube feeding are made by competent patients, counselors and/or chaplains can assist them in coming to grips with their diagnoses and in facilitating the process of determining how personal goals can be met by electing or rejecting specific medical interventions. Such patients have to decide what their priorities are and how they want to employ medical science in order to realize their goals. Undertakings of this kind can seem overwhelming for those who are ill and must face their physiological limitations. Skilled and sensitive counselors are able to provide an invaluable service as they help people sort through turmoil with the hope of finding peace.

Ideally family members should participate in the process in which competent patients engage. Physicians and counselors should make themselves available to serve family members. The management of treatment plans is much easier when loved ones understand and concur in the decision reached by a competent patient. In cases involving disagreement from family members regarding a patient's decision, family members could benefit from opportunities to express and examine the thoughts and feelings which give rise to the disagreement. They may also require help to comprehend why it is proper for them to respect decisions with which they continue to differ.

When a patient is incompetent it is appropriate that decisions regarding tube feeding be made by the patient's family. Ethicists Thomas A. Shannon and James J. Walter present the reasons why society entrusts this obligation to the family:

> The family typically plays an important role in these decisions, because often the individual most affected by a decision cannot participate directly. Such involvement is proper, because generally the family has a relationship with the patient and knows his/her wishes. The family is normally in the best position to discern the patient's wishes or desires. Thus it can either relate what the patient actually wanted or, failing that, relate its best judgment of what the patient would have wanted. If the family has no direct knowledge of the patient's wishes, it is still the appropriate

decision maker. The family has a socially recognized relation to the patient and can be presumed to have the best interests of the patient in mind.[5]

Regardless of what decision is reached about tube feeding, the process in which family members engage is emotionally draining. As we have seen, it takes time to accept the diminished existence of tube fed patients and it also takes time to be willing to forgo treatment and allow a patient to die. In the latter case, next of kin often find it necessary to initiate tube feeding so as to sustain their loved one by artificial nutrition for a time until they come to believe that it is right to let go. Physicians and other healthcare providers should respect the need to take time and should wait until next of kin are able to reach final decisions which they can live with. Establishing policies which make no distinction between discontinuance of tube feeding and its noninitiation will enable surrogates to take as much time as necessary to come to a decision.

It may happen that next of kin are unfamiliar with the medical technology of artificial feeding; as a result they may expect more from the technology than it can deliver. Accordingly, there may be a tendency to request all available medical interventions, including artificial sustenance, in the hope of restoring well being to a loved one. Only the first hand experience of seeing that the therapies bring no improvement will prompt the decision to discontinue treatment. A time-limited trial of tube feeding increases certainty regarding the prognosis and becomes a valuable source of information for the next of kin. Patience and compassion on the part of friends and healthcare professionals will make it easier for next of kin to pass through this difficult stage.

Sick and/or injured incompetents who cannot take nourishment by mouth and who are brought to a hospital emergency room are routinely tube fed. For those whose diagnosis reveals the impossibility of return to a cognitive, sapient state, artificial nutrition and hydration are generally understood to be dispensable by many moral authorities. It is hard for next of kin, however, to authorize discontinuance. They will probably have to deal with shock and disbelief, then with anger and disappointment before they will want to think about authorizing withdrawal of tube feeding. Support and comfort offered by people who realize the nature of their emotional struggles will help them to get through this sad time.

Psychological counselors who are on the staffs of hospitals and nursing homes can enable surrogate decision makers to work through their feelings. When next of kin are able to admit and articulate their feelings these feelings lose their disabling power. Angry, guilt-ridden, grief-stricken surrogates do not act rationally. Psychotherapists, chaplains and friends serve surrogates by helping them travel the road from emotional trauma to rational action.

Counselors should also be available to meet with family members in order to facilitate the task of reaching consensus. The professional skill of counselors is an invaluable asset to families which find it difficult to communicate. The patient direction of counselors can be instrumental in breaking deadlocks and resolving differences of opinion. It may happen, however, that in spite of the intervention of a counselor a family is unable to come to a decision which is acceptable to all. It is only in such a rare case that resolution would have to come through recourse to the courts.

Chaplains can serve surrogate decision makers by standing with them, supporting them through prayer, offering a sympathetic ear and a shoulder to cry on. Given the relative newness of the technique of artificial feeding and the lack of moral consensus regarding forgoing or withdrawing it (even in Catholic moral circles[6]) Catholic chaplains also serve by instructing surrogates as to the present state of the question. Fulfilling such a role requires that chaplains be willing to update themselves and be prepared to explain very complex subject matter in a way that is understandable to lay people.

Thus far in this section we have explored how patients or surrogates for incompetents can be assisted within a hospital or nursing home setting. Since both patients and surrogates also belong to the broader society it is fitting to explore the roles members of society should play in scenarios concerned with artificial feeding.

In general, distant relatives, friends, neighbors and coworkers need to be educated about the nature of dilemmas connected with artificial feeding so that they can be sympathetic and supportive to those facing decisions about the technology. A more particular challenge confronts members of two groups. Advocates of such diametrically opposed special interests as the pro-euthanasia right to die faction and proponents of the so-called right-to-life movement should regard each individual patient with respect and should resist the temptation to further their causes by manipulating sick and dying people. In regard to what may be a fundamental distortion of pro-life sentiment, Joseph J. Farraher, S.J., writes:

> In my judgment, . . . some pro-life people become [so] over-zealous in their fight against abortion and against euthanasia, that they go to the opposite extreme and may actually do more harm to the pro-life movement. Would that all of them would get a crash course on the papal and theological doctrine on extraordinary means. We should always remember that, although the prohibition against the deliberate and directly voluntary taking of the life of an innocent person is an absolute, the value of life on earth is not the greatest good in itself, but is a preparation for an infinitely better life hereafter. . . [7]

Father Farraher, standing within the Catholic tradition which advocates a consistent respect for life, reasons that this respect does not oblige the use of extraordinary means by those for whom such procedures hold no hope of recovery to health.

Persons who differ with pro-euthanasiast right to die advocates cite religious, moral, cultural and legal reasons for opposing overt acts of killing the sick or dying. They do not equate a willingness to let a gravely ill person succumb to his/her pathology with the willingness to sanction the killing of sick and dying patients.

Ministry to the Sick

The Catholic Church, through its ministry to the sick, provides a meaningful kind of support and assistance to patients on tube feeding. The Church's outreach also extends to healthcare professionals, family members and friends of the sick. This ministry is carried out by bishops and priests and by many other members of believing communities. Visiting the sick, sharing prayer and reflecting on the scriptures are some aspects of this ministry. Indicating the gift the sick give to those who love and care for them is another important part of this ministry. In the words of Pope John Paul II:

Let us keep the sick and handicapped at the center of our lives. Let us treasure them and recognize with gratitude the debt we owe them. We begin by imagining that we are giving to them; we end by realizing that they have enriched us.[8]

The most comforting aspect of the Church's ministry to the sick is the Sacrament of the Anointing. This sign of God's presence to suffering and incapacitated persons has been ritualized to include prayer, the laying on of hands and the anointing with oil. Bishops and priests are authorized by the Church to administer this sacrament. The sick, their relatives, friends and those who care for and minister to them find solace in receiving or witnessing the anointing. It is a vivid reminder of God's presence and God's will that each person ultimately come to wholeness. When reception of the Eucharist accompanies the Sacrament of the Anointing, the Eucharist is known by the name "Viaticum" because it is offered to a sick or dying person as food for the journey to heaven.

The Hardest Part of a Hard Decision

The hardest thing for a surrogate to have to clarify is the nature of what is omitted or withdrawn when an incompetent ward is not tube fed. Refusals to authorize the insertion of feeding tubes unfailingly result in the deaths of patients. If these patients do not die of malnutrition and dehydration *per se*, malnutrition and dehydration are a contributing cause of death. Offering food and drink to others, as well as sharing meals with them, hold profound social and symbolic meanings. There is a cultural expectation that able-bodied people will include feeding in the care they extend to vulnerable persons.

Surrogates who do not authorize tube feeding or who request its withdrawal come to comprehend silastic tubing, enteral and parenteral formulas, the artificial feeding process and the physiological sensations which accompany being tube fed in a different way from offering table food to a dependent person. It is very disturbing and frightening to imagine a loved one dying of thirst and starvation. If such were an accurate description of what is endured by an incompetent who is not tube fed, sensitive surrogates would probably always feel obligated to authorize tube feeding. The most crucial component of the hard decision to forgo or withdraw tube feeding is recognizing a difference between oral feeding and tube feeding and concluding that the latter is a medical treatment which may be refused or discontinuted if it offers no reasonable hope of benefit.

Conclusion

The beliefs which people hold influence their attitudes toward death and dying. Christian belief about immortality together with the common sense insight that for each person there comes an appropriate time to die point to a gracious letting go when there is no hope for recovery. Both patients who make their own decisions and surrogates who decide on behalf of incompetents find themselves in very stressful situations. The information and understanding provided by physicians, chaplains and counselors, as well as the support of relatives and friends, are much needed during such difficult times.

In regard to the technology of artificial nutrition and hydration, the toughest decisions fall to surrogates. Since this technology is now widely available and can be utilized in many different kinds of circumstances, it is important that the public-at-large learn about it. If competent adults were to take the initiative to educate themselves and formulate their intentions about artificial feeding should they become incompetent, their oral or written advance directives would considerably lessen the burdens borne by loved ones.

Endnotes

1. Eileen P. Flynn and Gloria Blanchfield Thomas, *Living Faith: An Introduction to Theology* (Kansas City, MO: Sheed & Ward, 1989), p. 396.

2. Cf., notes #17 and 18, Chapter One, and that to which they refer.

3. John Edward Ruark, M.D., Thomas Alfred Raffin, M.D., and the Stanford University Medical Center Committee on Ethics, "Initiating and Withdrawing Life Support," *The New England Journal of Medicine*, Jan. 7, 1988, 318:1, p. 25.

4. Ibid., p. 27.

5. Thomas A. Shannon and James J. Walter, "The PVS Patient and the Forgoing/Withdrawing of Medical Nutrition and Hydration," *Theological Studies*, December, 1988, 49:4, p. 646.

6. Ibid., pp. 623-647. Shannon presents the results of a survey he conducted of U.S. Catholic hierarchy on diocesan policies regarding authorization of nonfeeding

which showed that "different conclusions are drawn from this common heritage" and a "recognition that some consensus needs to be developed," p. 632. Points of disagreement are addressed in Chapter 3.

7. Joseph J. Farraher, S.J., "Questions Answered," *Homiletic and Pastoral Review*, May, 1988, p. 71.

8. Pope John Paul II, Homily given at Saint George's Cathedral, Southwark, London, May 28, 1982, in Charles W. Gusmer, *And You Visited Me: Sacramental Ministry to the Sick and Dying* (New York: Pueblo Publishing Company, 1984), p. 202.